plant this!

plant this!

Best Bets
for Year-Round
Gorgeous Gardens

ketzel levine
Illustrations by René Eisenbart

SASQUATCH BOOKS
SEATTLE

In memory of Sharon Millican
and Mary Notas, and in honor of my father,
Arthur Levine, who no longer has the word
for flower but remembers *La Bohème*.
—K. L.

In memory of my father,
whose love continues to sustain me.
—R. E.

Text ©2000 by Ketzel Levine
Illustrations ©Oregonian Publishing Co.
All rights reserved. No portion of this book may be reproduced or utilized in any form,
or by any electronic, mechanical, or other means without the prior written permission of the publisher.

The plant profiles in this book appeared in slightly different form in *The Oregonian* from 1997 to 1999.
Reprinted with permission of the Oregonian Publishing Co.

Published by Sasquatch Books
Printed in Hong Kong
Distributed in Canada by Raincoast Books, Ltd.
04 03 02 01   5 4 3

Cover and interior illustrations: René Eisenbart
Cover and interior design: Karen Schober

Library of Congress Cataloging-in-Publication Data
Levine, Ketzel.
  Plant this! / Ketzel Levine; illustrations by René Eisenbart.
     p. cm.
ISBN 1-57061-245-5 (alk. paper)
  1. Landscape plants—Northwest, Pacific. 2. Landscape plants—Northwest, Pacific—Pictorial works.
I. Eisenbart, René. II. Title.
SB405.5.67 L48 2000
635.9'51795—dc21   00-029653

Sasquatch Books
615 Second Avenue
Seattle, Washington 98104
(206) 467-4300
www.SasquatchBooks.com
books@SasquatchBooks.com

acknowledgments

During the past decade, my life has been charmed by botanically-possessed friends. Each has polished me up a bit, then passed me on to the next. I owe my first job outside radio to Joan Feely at the National Arboretum ($7/hr raking—a lateral move from public broadcasting), and my lasting love for trees and shrubs to Phil Normandy of Brookside Gardens (our crops are saved!).

Claire Sawyers of the Scott Arboretum inspired me to travel, and however inadvertently, prompted me and the dogs to head west. Thank you, Dan Hinkley and Robert Jones, for being here when we arrived.

For the keys to the city of Portland, I thank its true mayor, Sean Hogan, who, along with the aforementioned Hinkley, influenced much of this book. Others who added their spit and polish include Paul Bonine, Dan Heims, Jay Miner, Ernie and Marietta O'Byrne, Diana Reeck, Parker Sanderson, and Magi Treece.

I am indebted to the following authors, whose books are a constant in my life: Allan Armitage (*Herbaceous Perennial Plants*); Martha Barnette (*A Garden of Words*); Michael Dirr (*Dirr's Hardy Trees and Shrubs*); Arthur Lee Jacobson (*North American Landscape Trees*); Carole Ottesen (*The Native Plant Primer*); and Kim Tripp and the late J.C. Raulston (*The Year in Trees*). I wouldn't even have books if it wasn't for Debby Garman at Timber Press.

I waited twenty-five years for a boss such as JoLene Krawczak of *The Oregonian*. You should all be so blessed. I might also wish you a production editor as good as Novella Carpenter.

Now for the shmaltz: Neil Matteucci and Norm Kalbfleisch, but for your safe haven, who knows where I would have landed. Diana Ballantyne, Maggie and Sam Bittman, Cindy Carpien, Philip Hammond, Jay Miner, KymPokorny, Howard Shapiro, you are each a continued haven for my heart.

Finally, I gladly surrender the last words to Roz Levine: "The best thing I ever did was give you girls sisters." You're right, Mom. You did good.

—K. L.

I'd like to thank my family, both the Andreases and Eisenbarts. Your belief in me is the spring from where my creativity flows. Thanks to Ketzel Levine for her burning vision and to my friends at *Homes & Gardens of the Northwest* who have walked this path with me, especially Joany Carlin and JoLene Krawczak who gave me time to illustrate. Special thanks to all of you inside and outside *The Oregonian* who have encouraged me. Your words are the wind in my sails. I am grateful to Sandy Rowe and Fred Stickel for granting me permission to republish. And finally, thanks to Gary Luke, Karen Schober, and others at Sasquatch who have made my art into a real book.

—R. E.

contents

spring

summer

fall

winter

contents

On Choosing One Hundred Plants

I know, I know. Your favorite plant is not in this book. Now that we've confirmed my fallibility (what a relief), let's just talk.

I chose these one hundred plants using a variety of both valid and dubious criteria, emphasizing plants that were easy to please and exercising a decided prejudice in favor of those that would thrive in my own backyard. Given my tendency to anthropomorphize everything, I also chose plants as I might friends, including some that looked cool and some my heart went out to (i.e., ignored and undervalued plants), plus those I found either sexy, profound, or irrepressibly optimistic.

And just so you wouldn't feel alone, I also included a couple of plants I unwittingly tortured or destroyed (so much for the friend analogy). I thank the late J. C. Raulston for the great one-liner I now use to justify all dead plants (feel free to borrow it; see page 55).

As for choosing plants by their flower—well, given the fickle nature of beauty, I trust this ornamental feature least of all (a newly acquired philosophy, achieved when I hit forty-five). Which is not to say I'm perverse enough to covet a garden without bloom. But when you balance their capacity for transcendence with their utter unpredictability, flowers can break your heart. Obsessing over them is much like throwing yourself into an unstable relationship that has no real substance, only dizzying sex.

Fine, so grow plants for their flowers . . .

A couple of other points that bear thinking about as you peruse my hundred picks:

■ Hate me if you must, but I garden in the benign Pacific Northwest (USDA Zone 8). Though I've chosen many plants that are hardy to zero on the Fahrenheit scale, I've also included (and noted) ample fair-weather friends. Check with your local nursery or plant society if you've any doubt about a plant's suitability to your region (this includes its tolerance for heat and humidity, too).

plant this!

■ Plants are organized here under the season I think they look their best, not necessarily the one in which they flower.

■ A smear campaign against botanic Latin—denigrating it as highbrow—has blanketed much of the United States. Don't fall for it! It's about as highbrow as pig Latin, and a whole lot more fun. Here's how you play: Put your last name first and give it a botanic-speak ending, like "ia" or "us." Then replace your first name with a Latin word that describes something that sets you apart. For example, since I'm easily identified by my curly hair, my botanic name might be *Levineus spiralis*. Hollywood mermaid Esther Williams could be classified as *Williamsia aquaticus*, and the blue-eyed Paul Newman, *Newmanus azureus*. Get it? Now, you try.

■ Because dirt, to gardeners, is a benediction, I encourage you to baptize this book with filthy fingers, and make it your own by maligning me in the margins if you think I've left something out. The more opinionated and manure-ridden your margins, the more fun I'll know you're having. Which brings me to what I do hope you find in these pages: a respite from whatever ails you. Such was its writing for me.

spring

Arisaema

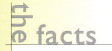

facts

BOTANICAL NAME:
Arisaema

SOUNDS LIKE:
Pasadena

COMMON NAME:
Jack-in-the-pulpit

TYPE:
Weird, tuberous
woodland perennial

BASIC NEEDS:
Part shade, adequate
moisture, humus-rich soil,
good to great drainage,
human blood

WORST ENEMY:
Bad drainage and poor,
parched soil

BEST ADVICE:
Mark where you put
your plants so you won't
inadvertently destroy them
in spring; mulch heavily
in late fall in more
extreme climates

A. ringens

Yikes! It's the Attack of the Aroids! It's the Arisaemas, chlorophyllic aliens in life forms resembling hooded cobras, miniature owls, and—according to one source who survived an encounter—men with "cute little ears that resemble a flustered Ross Perot." Wearing helmetlike spathes over their spiked spadices (more, later, on Alienwear), they are multiplying in numbers and stealing gardeners' souls.

It takes only one *Arisaema* to overpower any number of *Homo sapiens*. Not unlike a cobra, the plant hypnotizes its prey. It strikes by captivating the imagination, and the result is not pretty: Men and women of reason who were once happy enough growing flowers fast become acolytes of the Unholy Weird.

What's the allure? The improbability that plants like these can exist at all. From the ground up, they defy expectation: Stems wrapped in zigzagged snakeskins, and hooded flowers that fold back on themselves as if to protect an unspeakable secret. Some species have all but swallowed the evidence; out of their mouths dangle what seem to be the tails of hapless rodents that have taken a look-see and fallen right in.

The anatomy of all this weirdness breaks down into easily identifiable parts: The *spathe* is the leafy covering that encases the flower, and the *spadix* is the fleshy, clublike thing sitting inside (the "Jack" in the "pulpit"). The so-called mouse tail is the dental floss–like entrail at the ends of some spadices (plural of "spadix") or, in a few cases, at the end of the spathe. The entire ensemble often sits below the plant's leaves.

It's important that you know all this in order to identify the alien, because its general outward appearance varies considerably. Plants

A. candidissimum:
  Sweet-scented, pink-
  striped white spathe, as
  graceful as a calla lily;
  notoriously late to
  emerge, so be patient;
  16 inches

A. ringens:
  Glossy, trifoliate leaves;
  green-and-purple-striped
  spathe with purple lip;
  great view inside hood;
  12 inches

range from the eight- to eighteen-inch native Jack, *Arisaema triphyllum,* to the five-foot whipcord Jack, *A. tortuosum,* with a tail described by one eyewitness as looking like "the tongue of a tired bulldog." Single leaves can be multifingered and hover high in the air like umbrellas (*A. taiwanensis,* called the queen of the genus) or can look more like corrugated plastic rhubarb leaves in minty green (*A. griffithii,* with a cobra-headed flower about as sinister as an arisaema is ever likely to be).

Though the hooded beast is usually what undoes the victim (who then falls prey to bigger, uglier aroids such as the voodoo lily—but that's another story), some forms have enormous foliage appeal. *A. serratum* in particular is incredibly arresting: two hand-shaped green leaves highlighted by dramatic silver linings, perched on top of purple-patterned, reptilian stems.

Yet even if you've avoided infection by leaf, once the so-called flowers emerge, say goodbye to your reason. First you'll be seeing an owl face in the doubled-over spathe of *A. kiushianum*: a flat nose accented by two hoot-owl eyes. It's all very cute, considering. Next thing, you'll be stared down by the brooding purple *A. urashima* (syn. *A. thunbergii* var. *urashima*) and will find yourself snared by its whip of a spadix, which has been known to measure two feet long.

Arisaemas are way too clever to simply terrify or astonish their prey. One of the most beautiful species is not at all intimidating but impossibly luminescent in an alien way. *A. sikokianum* has a dark purple pitcher and a hood that's wide open—no tricks, no tendrils. But sitting inside is a small bald being surrounded by a pulsing white light, the kind you'd expect if you'd opened the lid of a buried treasure chest and found, inside, the Holy Grail.

Help! It's happening! I'm losing my grip! Quickly, then, I leave you with this whispered warning: If you open a plant catalog and see arisaemas listed, burn it immediately. The nurseryman is one of *them.*

Arisaema

Astrantia major

WOODLAND PERENNIAL

the facts

BOTANICAL NAME:
Astrantia major

SOUNDS LIKE:
Da rancha (Brooklynese
for "the rancher")

COMMON NAME:
Masterwort

TYPE:
Woodland perennial,
2.5 feet

BASIC NEEDS:
Sun to part shade, even
moisture, nice deep soil

WORST ENEMY:
Relentless sun, parched
soil, slug alert

BEST ADVICE:
Incredibly satisfying
for the beginner

Out of my way, *Astilbe*. I'm tired of your big hair. Besides, it's blocking my view of that demure looker beside you in the encyclopedia. No, not *Astilboides*, way too weird. I was thinking of sweet *Astrantia* — as do all gardeners who prefer flowers that beckon quietly then slowly reveal themselves to those who take the time to look. Maybe it's an aging thing, this disenchantment with ostentatious beauty, but humbler flowers — such as the masterwort — look better all the time. (Break your heart on enough Brad Pitts and you start kissing princes, hoping for a kind, sensitive frog.)

Handsome is precisely as handsome does, which is what makes *A. major* and its cultivars such astonishingly worthwhile plants. Not only are these woodland garden lovers easy to warm up to, they only feign homeliness. Fact is, these are deliciously showy plants.

What's misleading is the way their flowers resemble Queen Anne's lace (*Daucus carota,* same family), with tidbits of blooms displayed in a parasol-shaped cluster that makes you think "weedy." Once you are past this prejudice, each tidbit reveals itself as a constellation of tiny fertile flowers surrounded by a conspicuous collar of infertile bracts, the whole truth a complex and beguiling arrangement of cuteness, color, and form.

Consider the cultivar 'Hadspen Blood', selected by plantsfolk Nori and Sandra Pope at Hadspen House in England. It's a vigorous, mounding two-foot perennial with cut leaves reminiscent of hardy geraniums and a nonstop display of moody, dark-red flowers that vibrate above the foliage. Equal in value to the bloodiest *Dianthus,* they are a saturated color you don't expect in the shade.

Or let's talk about *A. major* subsp. *involucrata* 'Shaggy' (syn. 'Margery Fish'), a startling tritone job, with green-dipped white bracts, tinged pink near the base, at least twice as long as the compact flower cluster within. The overall effect is beguilingly bright; 'Shaggy' works like a footlight among taller plants.

Astrantias are no overnight sensations. Even as cut flowers, they can last two weeks. Otherwise, pinch flowers back to lateral buds and they'll often rebloom. Easygoing to the point of promiscuity, these moisture lovers will also self-seed; if you let them prolif-erate, you'll probably end up with every color but the one you started with, ranging from white through pink and on to ruby red.

Of course, the thought of an astrantia-mad garden may not delight you, in which case, after the second flush of pleasure, cut all flowering stems to the ground. Worry not that such action might dis-courage the courtship; this is a simple plant that mends hearts.

A. major
'Hadspen Blood'

'Buckland':
  Milky pink and sterile
'Lars':
  Dark red flowers, long
  green-dipped bracts
'Rose Symphony':
  Rosy pink flowers with
  silver collar of bracts
'Ruby Wedding':
  Dark red flowers, purple
  stems, darkish leaves;
  seedlings possibly more
  stable than 'Hadspen
  Blood'
**'Sunningdale
  Variegated':**
  Greenish white to pink-
  blushed flower; light
  green leaves splashed
  with creamy gold varie-
  gation, strongest in spring

A. maxima:
  Larger flowers, more
  rose-pink than white;
  intriguing 3-lobed leaves

Baptisia alba

SHRUBBY PERENNIAL

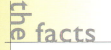

the facts

BOTANICAL NAME:
Baptisia alba (syn. *B. pendula, B. leucantha*)

SOUNDS LIKE:
Amnesia

COMMON NAME:
White false indigo

TYPE:
Shrubby, long-lived, late-spring perennial

BASIC NEEDS:
Full sun with fast drainage; supplemental summer water till established

WORST ENEMY:
Impatience; figure 4 years before it comes into its own

BEST ADVICE:
Great lupine substitute; forget transplanting

All I really needed to get through the last dark, wet spring was a stand of mature *Baptisia alba.* Not that I had one. The mail-order plant that arrived in late fall from South Carolina sat around unplanted till February (why am I admitting this?). The little bugger didn't show its head until mid-April, and for the next month was smaller than a slug—no doubt half the size of the slimy herbivore that promptly reduced it to a few maimed leaves.

But if I'd had a stand of those tall, dark, and slender smoky-purple stems that begin life looking like black asparagus shoots and by June are smothered in blindingly white, lupinesque flowers, I'm sure I would have laughed out loud at the weather's silly shenanigans. What kind of fool did May take me for, trying to pass itself off as November?

Except for one thing. No baptisia in its right mind would have come out to play in all that darkness. This robust and long-lived genus is native to dry, sandy woods, bright woodland edges and prairielike habitats in the East and Midwest. It lacks our good-humored Northwestern patience when it comes to going without sun.

I'm joking, of course. About our good humor. But I kid you not about the restorative powers of the false, or wild, indigo, which I'm prepared to describe as the most startlingly beautiful white-flowered perennial I know. Yes, I'd even trade six 'Casa Blanca' lilies for a good clump of *B. alba,* because I'm undone by the complexity of its beauty: delphinium splendor on a zaftig plant with both grace and taprooted stability.

Like its better-known blue relative, *B. australis*—once cultivated in the Southeast as a dye substitute for *Indigofera*—the white species has trifoliate gray-green leaves reminiscent of clover leaves, which are alternately arranged on extremely upright stems. The shrubby foliage of *B. alba* is said to hold up better through the season than that of *B. australis,* particularly in the South, but in less sunny locales the problem is more likely to be one of growth than wear and tear.

Even in ample sun, *B. alba* is slow to establish. Figure four years before you've got a mature clump. Given that I started mine in the sunny-spring-that-wasn't, I'm probably looking at five. The trade-off is that this plant has staying power, and it gets better (and more deeply rooted) with time. It's a good idea to plant it permanently and fill in with more mobile perennials while it lumbers along till three feet wide.

This exhaustive sales pitch notwithstanding, you also need to know about the cross between *B. alba* and *B. australis* that's named 'Purple Smoke'—a dark-legged beauty with a head of smoky violet blooms, introduced by the North Carolina Botanical Garden and Niche Gardens of Chapel Hill. I hesitate to shout too loudly because it's hard to get hold of, but guess what: So is the white wild form. All the more reason for you to join me in whining about its absence, in the hope that nursery folks will shut us up by giving this plant a try.

B. alba

gimme more

B. leucophaea (cream false indigo):
Creamy yellow flowers on earlier-blooming, laxer plant; takes it hot, dry, and well-drained; only 2 feet

B. tinctoria (yellow wild indigo):
Long, arching racemes of clear to cream yellow flowers; best in meadows

Baptisia alba

17

Berberis

B. × stenophylla

I always figured that most gardens were bereft of hot-blooded, orange-blooming *Berberis* because when people heard the word "barberry," they thought only of thorns. I decided to test this theory on my unsuspecting partner with a mind-probing word-association game:

"Daffodil," I said. "Yellow," he answered. "Rose," I suggested. "Pink," he replied. "Rhododendron?" "Green," he chortled.

"Okay, how about barberry?"

Long pause "Raincoat."

Looks like I figured wrong.

Evergreen barberries should only be so well known as the British trench coat. Instead, the berberis market has been flooded with the deciduous species from Japan, the bright-gold, rich-purple, and tricolored foliage forms that are grown by the gazillion coast to coast. What I'm pushing are the species from Chile, Tibet, and the Sichuan and Yunnan provinces of China, hardy to zero (the Japanese forms push –30°F) and colorful as *Crocosmia*.

For a close-up of the flowers, let's look at *Berberis darwinii*. It's a Chilean species discovered by Darwin in 1835, while he was voyaging on the HMS *Beagle* (my kind of boat). Here we have thumbnail-size bells arranged like a miniature cluster of cherries, each golden-orange flower hanging from a slender stalk. Even before the flowers open, the early spring effect is fantastic, with flame-colored buds set against dark, chunky, hollylike leaves on a six-foot eruption of foliage.

Another arching mass of orange is the species *B. linearifolia*. As the name suggests, the plant is identifiable by its long, narrow leaves. The spring blossoms, each nearly an inch wide, are displayed prominently along upright five-foot stems. Though the straight species is plenty showy, you might be on the lookout for the hybrid 'Orange King'.

the facts

BOTANICAL NAME:
Berberis

SOUNDS LIKE:
Burger kiss

COMMON NAME:
Barberry

TYPE:
Upright and arching evergreens with early spring flowers, 4 to 6 feet

BASIC NEEDS:
Soil and sun; doesn't get much easier

WORST ENEMY:
Nasty drainage

BEST ADVICE:
Full sun for best flowering

If orange sets your teeth on edge, evergreen barberries also bloom a delicious yellow, though one species has a peculiarly unappetizing name: *B. gagnepainii.* Monsieur Gagnepain's berberis blooms in small, light-yellow clusters, followed in fall by blue-blushed fruit. The foliage is quite distinctive, with wavy, undulating margins, giving this compact four-foot-by-three-foot shrub a striking texture year-round.

Also yellow-flowered is *B. verruculosa,* the warty barberry, with leathery, oval leaves and solitary, fat-budded blossoms smothering a nicely compact four-foot bush. Then there's *B. replicata,* a daintier beast with translucent burgundy new growth and narrow, wavy foliage like that of the "gag-me" barberry, made all the more effective by white undersides and daffodil-bright blooms.

Lastly, check out the vigorous and free-flowering hybrid, *B. × stenophylla,* which appears to have it all: very narrow, deep-green foliage with glaucous undersides; small but profuse, fragrant golden flowers; and an arching habit that works as well on a steep bank as it does in a hedge. Unfortunately, *B. × stenophylla* is too dense to hide under in case of sudden showers. For that kind of cover, you're better off with the hybrid, *B. × raincoat.*

gimme more

B. calliantha:
Dark, prickly leaves with brilliant white undersides, excellent red winter tones, and delicious lemon flowers. A vigorous 4-foot shrub from Tibet, and the biggest flowered species in the genus.

B. julianne:
Huge leaves; exceedingly hardy evergreen; great for the Midwest

B. x wisleyensis:
Graceful, lovely evergreen for shade

Berberis

Brunnera

B. macrophylla 'Langtrees'

the facts

BOTANICAL NAME:
Brunnera

SOUNDS LIKE:
Crooner uh

COMMON NAMES:
Heartleaf brunnera, false forget-me-not, Siberian bugloss

TYPE:
Spring-blooming perennial

BASIC NEEDS:
Part shade; rich, well-drained soil

WORST ENEMY:
Bad drainage, hot sun, drought

BEST ADVICE:
The straight species, *B. macrophylla*, is a foolproof beginner's plant

Quite a few Northwest gardeners are so inundated by the annual forget-me-not *Myosotis sylvatica* that they'd just as soon forget it. Yet even the most battle-weary can't deny that, for sparkle and vivacity, it's tough to beat the brilliance of forget-me-not blue.

Ms. Flora hankered something bad after the color blue, this much is clear. Witness the whole family, *Boraginaceae*, an embarrassment of azure riches from dawn sky to midnight blue. For the six of you obsessed with the borage blues, feast your eyes on the "gimme more" list.

If all you really want is the name of a stunning foliage plant with forget-me-not flowers, meet *Brunnera macrophylla* 'Langtrees'. I have here on my desk a one-year-old, four-inch pot of the plant, with no fewer than twenty-two African violet–sized leaves anxious to break out of the box. Even at this immature stage, it sports a big cluster of salt grain–sized blossoms tucked within the leaves, a cluster that might even flower if I'd quit picking the foliage apart.

The heart-shaped, gray-green leaves are covered with short hairs that make the plant look very fuzzy, but that's not what makes it shine. Instead, it's the irregular, brief brush strokes of metallic silver spots that adorn each leaf, aluminum highlights that will pop this plant out of the shade.

At maturity, the basal leaves of 'Langtrees' will be up to six inches across, no small presence among hostas, astilbes, and ferns. The plant can easily tolerate morning sun, does not need constant moisture, and, if happy enough to self-sow (which is by no means guaranteed), often comes true from seed.

That fact—along with the discouraging ones below—sets 'Langtrees' apart from the admittedly far more beautiful variegated brunneras. But the striking cultivar 'Variegata' (which some say is the same as 'Dawson's White') is an incredibly difficult plant to grow well, demanding just the right amount of light shade, plus evenly moist, well-drained soil (and if you'd be so kind, cancel the hot summer). Also, word on the block is that 'Variegata' is a highly unstable form. I've seen some three-year-old specimens of 'Variegata' that are decidedly more green than variegated.

I've also spied a couple of the exquisite Creamsicle cultivar 'Hadspen Cream', but I'm not going to say another word about this awesome selection because I've yet to find a U.S. source. Keep looking.

In defense of good old plain green leaves, you're bound to be delighted with the infinitely more affordable straight species, *B. macrophylla*. This one is a piece of cake to grow in morning sun to light shade, copes with occasional dryness once established, and makes impressive large-leaved mounds that get airier as they grow taller—waving the banner that much higher for forget-me-not blue.

gimme more

Not brunnera, granted, but related by their boraginaceous blue eyes:

Lithodora diffusa (typically 'Grace Ward'): Evergreen perennial; 6 inches; narrow dark green leaves; long-lasting azure blue flowers; sharp drainage, full sun

Myosotidium hortensia (New Zealand forget-me-not): Thick, fleshy stems and 2-foot glossy leaves; light blue flowers; hardy to 10°F, totally spectacular in pots

Omphalodes cappadocica (navelwort): Cultivars include 'Cherry Ingram' (large, deep-blue flowers), 'Starry Eyes' (deep blue flowers outlined in pinkish white), and 'Lilac Mist' (silvery mauve flowers); well-drained, even moisture, light shade; 14 inches

Omphalodes verna (blue-eyed Mary): Politely colonizes by underground stems; blue flowers with white throats; any soil, part shade; 4 inches

Ceanothus

EVERGREEN SHRUB

the facts

BOTANICAL NAME:
Ceanothus

SOUNDS LIKE:
Be a no fuss

COMMON NAME:
California lilac, wild lilac

TYPE:
Rounded, dense, spring-
blooming evergreen,
2 to 12 feet

BASIC NEEDS:
Sun, good to excellent
drainage, no summer water

WORST ENEMY:
Temperatures colder than
the low teens Fahrenheit

BEST ADVICE:
Prune hard and consistently
to keep wood young and
forgiving, in case the
shrub gets cut back
naturally by cold

I e-mailed a list of plants I wanted to grow to a colleague whom some say I idolize. I can't help it; I've never met anyone quite like Dan Hinkley, who doesn't just know plants but grows plants about as well as you're ever likely to see. My list passed muster, except for Mr. Hinkley's small editorial comment next to the genus *Ceanothus*:

"Yuck! Deciduous only!"

I was incredulous. The blue flowers on evergreen ceanothus, such as 'Dark Star' and 'Julia Phelps' were right up there with those of *Corydalis*, *Pulmonaria*, and *Lithodora*, except this time on a six-foot shrub. It was the West Coast native I'd most looked forward to growing ever since I'd moved to Portland. Deciduous? Was he actually advocating the white-flowered native *C. americanus*, that boring excuse for a ceanothus we were limited to back East?

"Clearly, you forget what life is like, blue-less, when all you can grow is that dumb white one from New Jersey," I wrote, not a little peeved.

"I like blue," he replied. "Just not blue combined with the crispy texture of burnt toast, which is what ceanothus leaves look like after 90 percent of our winters. And after three years of not dying back, they are too big to kill off if you wanted to. Yuck, yuck, double yuck."

Of all the nerve.

Mr. Hinkley's concerns about burnt toast have to do with his Kingston, Washington, environs, where winter temperatures are lower and longer and it's not quite hot enough in summer for plants to toughen up. Winter burn is less of a problem around Portland, but ever since Mr. Hinkley's attempt to burst my bubble, I have noticed that California lilacs lack a certain structural interest.

Fact is, they have a tendency to blob.

But what they lack in grace and movement, they make up for in foliage and flower: terminal clusters composed of countless tiny balloon buds that burst to reveal petals and pollen. Small, glossy, dark-green leaves add to the sparkle of these soothing blue blossoms, which catch the eye and draw you closer (without the ill effects of "azalea afterburn").

I just planted a cobalt-blue *C*. 'Concha' near the street on top of a retaining wall, a plant that's expected to reach six feet by six feet and eventually obscure all views. Gardeners with smaller spaces may find the ground-covering species easier to integrate, or may want to turn amenable varieties into casual espaliers (*C. impressus*, for example, or the pink-flowered cultivar 'Marie Simon'). Those with lots of space and sun can use the largest selections as a backdrop, sufficiently obscured so that the source is unclear if anyone smells burnt toast.

C. 'Concha'

First, the gorgeous blue-bloomed ever-greens:

'Dark Star':
Deerproof mounding shrub; profuse electric blue flowers; 6 feet

'Puget Blue':
Exceptional University of Washington cultivar

'Victoria':
Big back-of-the-border shrub; among the hardiest of this group; 6 to 10 feet

'Gloire de Versailles':
Semi-deciduous with larger, coarser leaves, to 12 feet; best if chopped hard to ground in spring (it'll still blossom for six weeks in late summer)

***C. gloriosus* (Point Reyes ceanothus):**
Mounding groundcover; lavender-blue flowers; easiest in well-drained soil

***C. gloriosus* var. *exaltatus* 'Emily Brown':**
Mounding to 2 feet, electric blue flowers

One Northwest native:

C. thyrsiflorus:
Tough 12- to 15-foot evergreen, mostly blue flowers; 'Snow Flurry' is a particularly heavy-blooming white

Ceanothus

23

Clematis macropetala

DECIDUOUS VINE

the facts

BOTANICAL NAME:
Clematis macropetala

SOUNDS LIKE:
Feminist back row peddler

COMMON NAME:
Clematis

TYPE:
Early-spring-flowering,
deciduous vine

BASIC NEEDS:
Part sun to dappled shade;
adequate moisture;
amended, well-drained soil

WORST ENEMY:
Wet feet

BEST ADVICE:
Don't sweat the pruning;
the vine's too small to
cause trouble. Trim long
shoots after flowering if you
don't like its shape

"Oh, goodness! How would you describe it?" Ask the clematis-struck Maurice Horn to tell you about the flowers on *Clematis macropetala*, and you can almost see him blush from the effort. "They start as tight, tiny oblong buds that just get bigger and bigger, the swelling is so exciting . . . the flower color is a subdued but luscious lavender blue, like nothing else in a climber this time of year . . . and the seed heads are fabulous—these fine, twisted threads becoming flight wings to be dispersed throughout the world!"

Delicate and ethereal? Look at them funny and they'll wilt? You don't know your *C. macropetala.* This species holds its own all the way up to the Arctic Circle ("mulched, of course," adds Horn) and is among the few clematis satisfactorily settled in Alaska. Native to northern China and Siberia, it's a rugged early-bloomer that's been there and done that before the harem girls of early summer even open their eyes (forgive me, Elsa, Nelly, and Betty).

Not that Maurice Horn is judgmental, mind you; the man cannot grow enough clematis. Joy Creek Nursery in Scappoose, Oregon, where Horn is part owner, is currently offering more than one hundred forms. What sets *C. macropetala* apart in his mind, though, is the way it can be used in the landscape, vining its way through ordinary garden shrubs just as their vibrant, fresh foliage arrives.

Timing is everything in the garden, which is precisely what *C. macropetala* has in its favor when it's used as a climber through Horn's preferred scaffold, *Pieris japonica.* "It's the combination of colors that really makes my heart beat," says Horn, who loves the look of the flowering clematis nestled in the foundation plant's brilliant emerging leaves. "Like a blue clematis with copper foliage." Now imagine those same flowers blinking through the blinding young red leaves of photinia. Sort of scary, huh?

The reason *C. macropetala* is best grown through shrubbery is that the six- to ten-foot vine isn't all that interesting come June ("They lack charm," admits Horn). But let it work its way through, say, a double file viburnum as the chartreuse foliage emerges, and the vine will conveniently disappear just as the horizontally tiered shrub fills out.

Given that *C. macropetala* and its cultivars take everything from sun to dappled shade, all you need in a host shrub is an accommodating shape. Nandinas, for instance, are too upright; rhodies are too dense, and they also lack the exciting spring foliage that *C. macropetala* needs to really show off. Shrub roses will work if you promise to trim them only lightly, lest you leave your enchanted April clematis all dressed up with no place to grow.

C. macropetala

'Jan Linkmark':
  Bicolored effect from inner whitish and outer violet-purple sepals
'Markham's Pink':
  Strong, glowing, clear pink
'Maidwell Hall':
  Wisteria blue
'Rosy O'Grady':
  Rosy purple; once readily available, now hard to find
'Floralia':
  Subdued pale blue

Note:
  The white-flowered forms are thought to be far less robust and more difficult to grow.

Clematis macropetala

Corydalis

C. flexuosa 'Père David'

the facts

BOTANICAL NAME:
Corydalis

SOUNDS LIKE:
Or riddle this

TYPE:
Impossibly blue, spring-blooming perennial

BASIC NEEDS:
Bright shade to part sun, good drainage, even moisture, rich soil

WORST ENEMY:
Drying out; −0°F temperatures

BEST ADVICE:
Try several, keep the tags, see what works, and go back for more; best massed

Every great plant deserves a story, and *Corydalis flexuosa*, the blue-eyed box-office hit of the decade, comes with a good one. Since I can't possibly improve on the way Graham Rice tells the tale in his book *Hardy Perennials*, I'll pass his telling along. The story opens in 1989 with three Englishmen—James Compton, John d'Arcy, and Martin Rix—on a plant expedition in western China.

"Frustration mounted as they were driven through dappled woods past startling sheets of blue, until the reluctance of their Chinese hosts to pause and allow the team to inspect the plants so inflamed their bladders that an urgent stop was insisted upon, during which time three small pieces of [*Corydalis*] rhizome were secreted in a moss-lined film canister. . . . A certain amount of subterfuge was necessary to ensure their introduction."

To say the least, the secret's out. In the past decade, those three stem snippets have been propagated into untold millions of plants

spring

under three cultivar names: 'Purple Leaf', 'Père David', and 'China Blue'. Each makes a low-growing, compulsively tidy groundcover with finely dissected foliage, topped by a cluster of upright, spurred blossoms that could turn turquoise to envy and rival the color of Paul Newman's eyes.

The differences among the three are subtle but worth noting, though all are choice woodland plants. 'Purple Leaf' has the best year-round foliage, with dark stains at the base of each leaflet. Though its flowers are somewhat less electric than those of the other two cultivars, it is unfazed by winter and is the earliest to bloom.

The rich, turquoise-tinged flowers of 'Père David' are the largest of the trio's (mind you, we're talking eighths of an inch), nodding above blue-green foliage on mahogany stems. This cultivar can produce sizable colonies, spreading by underground stems. 'China Blue' is the truest, brightest shade of a New England winter sky, and asks the same cultural conditions as the others: light shade, rich soil, and adequate moisture.

With the floodgates now open, nurseries are increasingly awash in this bleeding-heart relative (which means prices are coming down; I once paid twelve dollars for a four-inch pot!). Of late there's 'Blue Panda', awarded the highest azure prize of all for flowers that are *Meconopsis* (blue poppy) blue. I'm also high on the straight species, *C. elata*, with purple airbrushed flowers. If you're close enough to the ground, you'll find them sweetly fragrant; I've also found the plant singularly robust.

Bloom time for all these baby blues is anywhere between March and June, then perhaps October and, who knows, maybe into winter. Quite impressive, but I wouldn't say unstoppable, since a number will go dormant in summer and disappear without a trace. That's a little unnerving if you've a rotten memory, so consider leaving their tags in the ground. Film canisters will work, too.

gimme more

CREAM TO YELLOW

C. cheilanthifolia:
Ferny leaved, finely dissected foliage on nearly stemless plant; seeds liberally in rock walls

C. lutea:
Golden-yellow flowers resembling fringed bleeding heart; yes, it self-sows, but we should all have such problems

C. ochroleuca:
Creamy flowers with green lips atop blue-green foliage; prolific bloomer; nearly evergreen in Northwest

PINK

C. scouleri:
Large-leaved, graceful 2 to 3 feet with spike of rich pink flowers clustered along stem; needs even moisture, shade; native to northwestern Oregon

C. sempervirens (rock harlequin):
Feathery mounds of gray-green foliage, pink flowers with yellow tips; self-seeding biennial

C. solida (fumewort):
Low mats of deeply cut, grayish foliage and squat racemes of pinkish-lilac flowers in spring; summer dormant; plant bulbs in fall; full sun

Corydalis

Enkianthus

DECIDUOUS SHRUB

the facts

BOTANICAL NAME:
Enkianthus

SOUNDS LIKE:
Send me Kansas

COMMON NAME:
Red-vein enkianthus

TYPE:
Narrow, upright, lightly
textured spring-blooming
deciduous shrub;
6 to 15 feet

BASIC NEEDS:
Light shade; even moisture;
rich, well-drained soil

WORST ENEMY:
Will not tolerate drying out

BEST ADVICE:
Site at the edge of a
path so you can observe
flowers close up

I've been watching my parents' *Enkianthus* die for the last three years. It has not been a pretty sight. I keep thinking back to the plant I'd given them, a beautifully proportioned little shrub, with tiers of foliage ringing with rosy-belled blossoms and a bonfire of color in fall.

Alas, all that remain are a lot of twigs and a couple of leaves. Consider this, then, a eulogy; next time I'm back East visiting my parents, it's time for the old heave-ho. One thing enkianthus can't ever forgive is a lack of water, and one thing my dad never had much time for was the long, saturating soak.

The plant they've got is the unimproved species, *E. campanulatus*, which I'd hoped might reach eight feet in their lifetime but has barely inched past three feet. Related to the rhododendron, red-vein enkianthus has an elegant, upright habit of layered branches with tufted foliage crowded at the ends of the stems. A friend of mine likens it to the particularly gorgeous *Rhododendron quinquefolium*, an elegant creature whose leaves are in whorls of five. High praise indeed for the enkianthus, which is a whole lot easier to find, and at a fraction of the cost.

The flowers on the straight species are perhaps the least interesting (I am a good daughter, honest; I just couldn't find any cool cultivars at the time)—pendulous, creamy vanilla cups streaked red. The petals of the flower swell at the base, a subtle but telling feature, since *Enkianthus* can be translated as "pregnant flower."

Richer-veined varieties such as 'Red Bells' pack a little more *oomph* than does the species. So does the solid-pink form, 'Showy Lantern', while the maroon-budded 'Sikokianus', with shrimp-pink

E. perulatus:
'Compactus':
Exceptional miniature
specimen, barely 2 feet
after 25 years, perfect
for the ever-patient rock
gardener
'Lyddon J. Pennock':
Award-winning cultivar
with fabulous red fall
color

veins on brick-red flowers, makes a particularly impressive show. If you're after red, though, I've seen pictures of a species that seems to blow other forms out of the water. *E. cernuus* var. *rubens* (syn. *E. cernuus* var. *masudae* f. *rubens*) has long, nodding clusters of saturated red blossoms, more easily believable as clusters of fruit than as flowers. Personally, I like my enkianthus white because they read so well from a distance. The species of the above form, *E. cernuus*, is a pretty eight- to ten-foot flowering shrub with bright, showy racemes. My parents' plant comes in a pale form, too: *E. campanulatus* 'Albiflorus', with greenish-white, lily-of-the-valley cups. But the finest snowy-white display has got to belong to the incredibly refined species *E. perulatus*, which slowly tops out at about five to six feet high and wide, and possesses all the grace and intrigue of a dwarf elm. But hey, why stop there? In a genus that's known for stunning autumn color, I've heard enticing rumors that the foliage of this species is the most brilliantly red of them all.

E. campanulatus

Epimedium

WOODLAND PERENNIAL

When the first-century botanist Dioscorides named *Epimedion*, he was actually describing a different beast than the *Epimedium* we know today (I haven't a clue what plant he was describing). This nomenclatural snafu makes a certain amount of sense when you consider the contradictions embodied by this plant.

The foliage of epimedium, or barrenwort, appears timid as it unfolds—diminutive, heart-shaped leaves suffused with an embarrassed red blush. Its flowers are impossibly dainty, hovering in midair on thread-thin stems, giving rise to cutesy common names such as "fairy wings."

Yet the plant is an absolute bear—long-lived, shade-tolerant, and willing to cohabit with tree roots. Fact is, it's positively virile. Check out this ad I found for an herbal stimulant made from epimedium leaves (honest, I did not make this up):

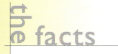

the facts

BOTANICAL NAME:
Epimedium

SOUNDS LIKE:
Stop the tedium

COMMON NAMES:
Barrenwort, bishop's hat, fairy wings

TYPE:
Spring-blooming perennial, evergreen to deciduous, depending on zone

BASIC NEEDS:
Light to full shade; water until established; well-drained soil

WORST ENEMY:
Short of pan-frying these woodland lovers, you can't go wrong

BEST ADVICE:
Even on evergreen species, cut ratty leaves back to ground in February so you get a better view of the diminutive blossoms

E. × rubrum

"Tired of always feeling insecure? Passive? 'MANHOOD' will get rid of the female feelings and let the totally cool, aggressive, powerful man you really are come out smokin'!"

An herb for the yang at heart.

But it would be a fabulous waste of foliage to harvest epimedium, a plant whose versatility as an ornamental rivals such stalwarts as pachysandra and vinca. Consider the evergreen workhorse *Epimedium × versicolor* 'Sulphureum', which—once established—forms a dense mass in that great nemesis, dry shade. Like many epimedium species, its young leaves are mottled red, a nice contrast to its early sunshine blooms.

Also unbeatably tough is *E. pinnatum* subsp. *colchicum*, parent to 'Sulphureum', a large, glossy-leaved native from northern Iran with bright citrus-yellow flowers. *E. alpinum* 'Shrimp Girl' is another ruffian at half the height: a tight, eight-inch clump of toothed, dark-green leaves, topped by columbine-like lemon spurs and red petals.

E. × perralchicum is an unstoppable colonizer (this is a good thing), generally represented by the robust, bright-yellow 'Frohnleiten', with sassy one-inch flowers. Also vigorous but harder to find is *E. davidii*, a recent introduction from China's Sichuan province that looks amazing on the page: dark-red stems balancing primrose- yellow blossoms, reminiscent of airborne helicopters (or Jughead's cap?).

White, pink, lavender, violet, even orange—all are represented in the genus, but I've saved the last word for the rosy red deciduous species, *E. × rubrum*. The flowers are delightful, but you grow this one for the leaves, which emerge as tender, light-green valentines delicately edged in red. The foliage is so perfect it's enough to make you weep—assuming you haven't overdosed on "Manhood."

gimme more

Here are a few non-yellow choices:

PINK THROUGH PURPLE
E. acuminatum:
Lavender to purple; sometimes huge, always spiny-edged, evergreen leaves

E. 'Enchantress':
Rosy lavender; evergreen corrugated leaves with white undersides

E. grandiflorum 'Lilafee':
Deep violet flowers, paler spurs; glossy purple new growth

E. leptorrhizum:
Largest of all flowers, to 6 inches; recently introduced species

RED-ORANGE
E. x warleyense:
Large coppery red; semi-evergreen, colonizing and tough

WHITE
E. grandiflorum 'White Queen':
Pristine large, cupped flowers with long spurs; deciduous

E. grandiflorum var. higoense:
Young leaves with distinct dark red margin; smaller plant

Epimedium

Euphorbia

the facts

BOTANICAL NAME:
Euphorbia

SOUNDS LIKE:
Euphoria

COMMON NAME:
Spurge

TYPE:
Perennial, blooms late winter through spring; 15 inches to 4 feet

BASIC NEEDS:
Full sun (with exceptions), extremely well-drained soil

WORST ENEMY:
Soggy soil; some species resent the approach of 0°F

BEST ADVICE:
Some euphorbias are extremely aggressive (e.g., *E. cyparissias*, the cypress spurge), choose wisely; also, because euphorbia's milky sap is toxic, gardeners with sensitive skin should wear gloves; all who handle the plant should take care not to rub their eyes

Eureka, euphoria, *Euphorbia!* If ever there was a genus to celebrate, this one's it. It's more than just part of the plant family *Euphorbiaceae,* it's part of the family of man.

It was known in Julius Caesar's Rome, it was known to the Oubangu tribes of the Congo, and it shows up annually on the display aisles of your nearest Safeway. What? Ever hear of a poinsettia? It's *Euphorbia pulcherrima!* I'm telling you, where there's life, there's euphorbia.

Of course, you'd have to be a euphorbiologist to know when you were looking at one, because the genus comes in innumerable sizes and forms. The Romans' euphorbia was a Mediterranean succulent, and the Oubangus' was a tall, spiny shrub. Travel the tropics of East Africa, and you'll find tree forms of euphorbia ninety feet high.

Sadly, by comparison, the range of euphorbs that will work in our gardens is minuscule. We've got only a few hundred really good ones from which to choose. Don't panic. I'm limiting myself to just five.

If you've ever complained that groundcovers for dry shade lacked enthusiasm, meet the wood spurge *Euphorbia amygdaloides* var. *robbiae.* It has rounded, glossy, dark-green leaves that make a tight, spreading fifteen-inch mound, pristine and buoyant through winter. Even in the driest, deepest shade, you can count on cheery panicles of yellow flowers high above the foliage in early spring.

E. dulcis 'Chameleon'

About that same time, in the sunnier part of the garden, *E. dulcis* 'Chameleon' is just waking up, looking as rich as chocolate pudding in contrast to April's veggie-green. The flavor lasts for months, and can be had again by cutting the plant back in early summer (or right after flowering to keep this notorious self-seeder in check). My guess is you've seen—and wanted—this addictive plant, which now

E. amygdaloides 'Purpurea'

tops the charts among purple-leaved perennials. Not half bad for a rogue picked up in a shady French ditch.

The species *E. characias* comes in two sun-loving subspecies: var. *characias* and *wulfenii* (hey, I'm just the messenger). They share a few general characteristics: three- to five-foot arresting architecture with long arching stems, bluish-green leaves, and bold yellow flower heads. Both have many named varieties, each with slightly different attributes, including the more dwarf 'Humpty Dumpty', the bluer 'Jade Dragon', and the lusciously upholstered 'Portuguese Velvet', my favorite 'phorb for foliage.

Among the several orange-red–flowered species in the family, I'd recommend *E. griffithii* 'Dixter', which never seems to have a dull moment: purple-orange shoots, red stems, bronzed foliage, and burnt apricot–orange flowers. At its best in richer soil, this Christopher Lloyd selection is typically euphorbic and may decide it needs more of the bed. But as is the case with all the plants I mentioned, you can keep 'Dixter' in check by yanking out unwanted plants as soon as they emerge.

Okay, so I snuck in more than five. But I'll bet you can't grow just one.

E. amygdaloides var. *robbiae*

E. amygdaloides:
'Purpurea'
  Purple-red leaves, lime green flowers
'Rubra':
  Richly colored winter foliage

E. x martinii:
  Rich purple stems, gray-green leaves

E. myrsinites:
  Succulent, blue-gray trailer; likes hot crevices and walls

E. polychroma:
  Impressive conical flower heads, rich purple stems
'Major':
  Very early yellow flowers; great fall color
'Midas':
  More compact, just as brilliant

Euphorbia

Halesia

A lone tree stands in a nursery in Portland with pendulous white bells ringing from its arms. You'd think someone might listen. But there it sits, unnoticed, choked by cherries and smothered by lilacs, with dogwoods baying to its lonesome tune.

Let's face it, if a plant trades in subtlety yet blooms in midspring, odds are good it won't get noticed. That's the only way I can explain why we don't grow more of the American native *Halesia,* which hit the shores of England decades before those rumors that we were using harbors to steep our tea.

The Carolina silverbell, *H. carolina* (syn. *H. tetraptera*), was the first halesia grown abroad. Commonly called silverbell, it's native not only to its namesake state but as far south as Florida and west to Oklahoma. Largely found on woodland edges, particularly along streams, *H. carolina*—much like redbud and dogwood—is a classic understory tree.

In the landscape, though, this silverbell functions more as a huge, low-branched shrub with several trunks, forming an open, transparent structure almost as wide as it is tall. Its mature bark is strikingly veined in gray and black, and its pest- and disease-resistant leaves are pleasantly oval. Come winter, its showy, four-winged fruits (hence the name *H. tetraptera*) dangle like deflated punching bags, and are often fodder for birds.

But for ten days in spring, the silverbell is no less than a benediction for humanity, with white, breathless bells that hang on angel hair–thin stalks and seem to enlighten anyone or anything beneath them. These simple, joyous flowers are the epitome of how I visualize faith: exquisitely simple and awesome in power.

Yup, they're that good.

Like faith, however, they're fleeting; once they're gone, it's hard to believe they ever happened. Of course, one could say the same about Kwanzan cherries and lilacs, whose flowerless branches lack the

the facts

BOTANICAL NAME:
Halesia

SOUNDS LIKE:
Rhodesia, or Rhodie zheeya

COMMON NAME:
Silverbell

TYPE:
Multiple-stemmed or low-branched, small, rounded tree; to 25 feet

BASIC NEEDS:
Sun to part shade, well-drained, evenly moist soil

WORST ENEMY:
Nasty drainage

BEST ADVICE:
Be sure this gets supplemental summer water; great East Coast substitute for the blight-infected dogwood
(*Cornus florida*)

slightest inspiration. What does last with silverbell is a canopy of foliage that provides a perfect shelter for smaller rhodies and azaleas.

Having maxed out on sublimity, I now lack the adjectives to describe the later-flowering *H. diptera* var. *magniflora,* a selection of the two-winged (hence the name *diptera*) silverbell that is—at last!—increasingly available in the trade. This often multistemmed variety has larger and more abundant blossoms than *H. carolina* (at one and a half inches, twice the size) and deeply cut, delicate lobes. The tree itself is slightly smaller, and its later bloom time gives it an edge on the competition.

But whether it's the two- or four-winged creature, siting is everything when it comes to the silverbell. Consider planting one at the edge of a path, on top of a slope, over a patio, or outside a window—anyplace where it won't be overlooked when the moment of benediction comes.

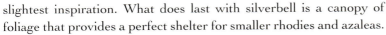

gimme more

Here are a few, but there's no guarantee on easy availability:

H. carolina 'University of Connecticut Wedding Bells': Oversized white flowers; very floriferous; to 20 feet

H. monticola: Larger cousin, makes a good shade tree; to 60 feet

'Rosea': Pale pink flowers; to 50 feet

'Variegata': Creamy variegation; very new to the trade

H. carolina

Variegated Iris

BULBOUS PLANT

the facts

BOTANICAL NAME:
Iris (variegated forms)

SOUNDS LIKE:
Virus

TYPE:
Rhizomatous perennial

COMMON NAME:
Iris

BASIC NEEDS:
Full sun to shade; thirst
varies among species

WORST ENEMIES:
Slugs and snails

BEST ADVICE:
The single most impressive
workhorse evergreen in my
garden is *I. foetidissima*
'Variegata'; it has flourished
in shade and with
precious little water

The goddess Iris was an Olympian messenger, and boy, was she a hoofer. Day after day, she walked the rainbow that bridged heaven and earth. As you might expect, with all that walking, she often picked up rainbow pieces on the soles of her feet, so that wherever she walked on earth, her footprints bore flowers in all the colors of the rainbows she'd traveled. We call those flowers iris.

From time to time, though, our Iris would overdo it on the nectar, cross the rainbow's median strip, and pick up white or yellow lines. Eventually, those lines showed up in the plants' leaves. We call those plants variegated iris.

What, you'd rather have me tell you that the variegation in an iris is either a genetic mutation or a disfiguring plant virus? Tough way to sell you a plant!

Like most variegated plants, the striped iris are grown for their foliage rather than for their flowers—which is a good thing in the case of the exquisite though unreasonably rare *Iris foetidissima* 'Variegata', since its pale mauve flowers are unlikely to attract attention. All the better, though, to enjoy its dramatic eighteen-inch evergreen leaves, brilliant fans of white-streaked foliage that blend with anything in summer, bring drama to winter, and thrive in shade.

Iris pallida 'Argentea Variegata' is another stunner, this one with showier lilac-blue flowers that smell like grape juice. Its flat, blue-green foliage striped silvery white remains interesting spring through fall, in either sun or light shade. Incidentally, the Latin word *argentea* means "silver," an important point to remember when shopping for *Iris pallida*, because another variety, 'Aurea Variegata', is the same plant striped with yellow. Choosing between the two is largely a question of aesthetics and of which works better in your garden.

In the category, Variegated Iris with Most Dramatic Flower, the winner is *Iris laevigata* 'Variegata', familiarly known (in which circles I know not) as "variegated rabbit ears." Midnight-purple flowers jump out from a three- to five-foot plant known for its particularly clean variegation. It's happiest with its head in the sun and its feet moist or sopping wet.

Perhaps the finest of the standing-water iris is the big and bold *I. pseudacorus* 'Variegata', incredibly easy to grow and amazingly satisfying in flower, its bright-yellow blooms echoed in its arching, striped, five-foot leaves. The variegated yellow flag is virescent (meaning that its leaves revert to green by summer), but that should not dissuade you from including it in your pond for its overall exuberance and reliable spring show.

Incidentally, when that roving goddess cooled her feet in American lakes and marshes, she left us with a superb selection of native water-loving iris. By that time, though, she'd laid off the nectar; to date, none of our natives have road-striped leaves.

I. pallida 'Argentea Variegata'

Pacific Coast Iris

BULBOUS PLANT

the facts

BOTANICAL NAME:
Iris (Pacific Coast natives)

SOUNDS LIKE:
Virus

COMMON NAME:
Pacific Coast iris

TYPE:
Primarily evergreen perennials from rhizomes

BASIC NEEDS:
Part sun, no summer water, well-drained soil

WORST ENEMY:
Human handling; single-digit weather

BEST ADVICE:
For minimal root damage, handle before bloom or in mid-fall, forget dividing

So we've already met Iris the Olympian messenger, who walked the rainbow bridging heaven and earth and tracked pieces of rainbow on the soles of her feet. Later in that same myth . . .

It wasn't long before a bunch of savvy nursery people began bagging the biggest chunks of rainbow our goddess left behind and marketing them as "bearded iris." Not surprisingly, she took offense—"My facial hair is not funny!"—and deliberately set off to find a place on earth where people were gentle and kind. Her bashful, tiptoed traces can still be seen in the magic land of Oregon, where the gentle people call them Pacific Coast iris, or "P.C.I.s."

I. 'Banbury Beauty'

Iris, however, neglected to tell the good Oregonians that it was all right to spread the word about her diminutive gems, and being by nature a reticent folk, they kept quiet about what they had. The goddess felt unjustly ignored—particularly since she'd outdone herself with attention to detail—so she cursed the P.C.I.s by making them hell to establish, and moved to Siberia where people were grateful for whatever they could get.

Come back, Iris! It was all a misunderstanding! We simply didn't want to dig your treasures out of the wild. But we've got them in cultivation now, in every conceivable hue, with veins so delicate they seem to pulse with your life, on multihued petals worthy of your name.

"Pacific Coast iris" is the catchall name for about a dozen different species found west of the Cascade Mountain range. Southern Oregon's Siskiyou Mountains are home to the largest concentration of P.C.I.s, including *I. douglasiana, I. innominata,* and *I. chrysophylla,* all promiscuous perennials that cross freely among themselves to create stupendous hybrids. (They cavort just as shamelessly in the home garden, too, an incredible bonus if you're into diversity; better not let them go to seed if you want your cultivars pure.)

The characteristics that distinguish the P.C.I.s from many other garden irises are their diminutive size—generally, under a foot and a half—and the complicated pastel range of their colors, from pale creamy yellows to rich mustards and from sky- to sea-blues through purples. Most have long, narrow, grasslike blades (*I. douglasiana*'s are the most voluptuous), that remain crisply evergreen, and flowers etched lovingly with contrasting colored veins. Though not the earliest of the iris to bloom (the dwarf forms beat them), they can be as much as a month ahead of the beardeds and the Siberians, and because of their size and year-round arching foliage, they are easy minglers in the garden.

First, though, you must coax them into staying—no easy feat after Iris cast her moody spell and gave the plants unforgivingly tender roots. P.C.I.s hate to be transplanted and divided, so you need to be especially kind. "Leave 'em and love 'em!" says Barbara Aitken, co-owner of Aitken's Salmon Creek Garden in Vancouver, Washington, one of the few Northwest nurseries (not to mention mail-order catalogs) offering these breathless beauties. After ample heartbreak, Aitken is all too familiar with their downright contempt for disturbance and recommends paying homage to these irises by planting them in a permanent shrine.

I. douglasiana:
White through deep blue-stained flowers; broad-leaved robust clumps

I. innominata, golden iris:
Gently ruffled pale to deep yellow and apricot flowers

I. chrysophylla:
Pale creams through mustard yellow

I. tenax:
Lavender to dark purple; most northerly of P.C.I.s, and often deciduous

Pacific Coast Iris

Lychnis

the facts

BOTANICAL NAME:
Lychnis

SOUNDS LIKE:
Sickness

COMMON NAMES:
Maltese cross (L. chalcedonica), rose campion (L. coronaria), or German catchfly (L. viscaria)

TYPE:
Brilliantly colored biennial or short-lived perennial

BASIC NEEDS:
Full to afternoon sun, good drainage

WORST ENEMY:
Shade and mucky soil

BEST ADVICE:
Plan ahead for what else will be flowering when the screaming neon rose campion hits her stride

If, as Ralph Waldo Emerson wrote, "Earth laughs in flowers," then the genus *Lychnis* has got one hee-haw. If it were a woman, she'd be the type Seinfeld would date for her figure; then, once she opened her mouth, he'd run screaming from the room.

His loss, as always. The genus *Lychnis*, once in flower, can make a party. The challenge is choosing the right kind of company—those not easily offended—because this is one performance you don't want to waste.

The white-and-woolly-leaved *L. coronaria*, known familiarly as rose campion, flowers in a shade of magenta so bright it's been described as floral original sin. Its common name is thought to be derived from the word "champion" because its blossoms were used to make garlands for sporting heroes. Its genus name—from the Greek, meaning "lamp"—refers to the use of its leaves, in ancient times, as candle wicks (as if the flowers alone couldn't light the way).

Short-lived and self-seeding (you noticed, huh?), drought-tolerant and best in full sun, *L. coronaria* has a screaming presence that works with a surprising number of other colors: grays, lilacs, and purples; blues and other magentas; bright yellows if you've got a sense of humor; and silver and white variegated leaves such as those of *Miscanthus* 'Morning Light'. It even looks good with its tamer twin, the cultivar 'Alba', which has the same strong upright habit and *Verbascum*-like rosettes of fuzzy leaves.

L. chalcedonica, the Maltese cross or Jerusalem cross, is less interesting in leaf and habit than rose campion but has a zinging color and is just as hot to trot. Named after the symbol used by the Knights of St. John of Jerusalem, an eleventh- and twelfth-century charitable order, the flowers make a dense head of bright scarlet atop upright, hairy stems. Some say the plant's nondescript foliage is a lot to put up with for a relatively small flower, but it's an old-fashioned favorite that continues to outlast its critics and enchant lovers of red.

The German catchfly, *L. viscaria*, offers a better balance of foliage and flower, forming clumps of dark green, grassy foliage and late-spring flower spikes with magenta blossoms. Its common name refers to its sticky stems. I've read about quite a large selection of double-flowered cultivars (including the bright pink 'Flore Pleno'), but I can't say I've seen them in the trade. Admittedly, I haven't knocked myself out trying.

And for the trendiest lychnis making the rounds today: *L. × arkwrightii* 'Vesuvius', a recent pinup in *Horticulture* magazine, with chocolatey purple-stained leaves and loud orange flowers. I've maligned this plant for its temperamental, less-than-exuberant habit, but watching its foliage emerge this spring, I got the point. Seeing 'Vesuvius' mixed with the bronze-leaved *Crocosmia* 'Solfaterre' and the *Coleus* 'Rustic Orange' is well worth the price of admission, even if the performance doesn't last.

L. × arkwrightii 'Vesuvius'

gimme more

L. x *arkwrightii* 'Orange Gnome':
A pint-size 'Vesuvius', to 8 inches

L. *cognata*:
Tough and longer-lived; melon flowers on lax stems; to 16 inches

L. *chalcedonica* var. *rubra-plena*:
Double scarlet-red form of Maltese cross; hard to find

L. *flos-cuculi* (ragged robin):
Narrow, grasslike foliage and deeply cut, ragged petals; for naturalizing in wet and wild places

'Rosea Plena':
Double pink to deep rose flowers

L. *flos-jovis* (flower of Jove):
Rosettes of woolly gray foliage with loose heads of muted purple-pink flowers; likes poor, well-drained soil; to 1 foot

'Minor':
Bubblegum-pink flowers; 8 inches

Lychnis

Magnolia

FLOWERING TREE

M. sieboldii

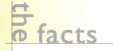

the facts

BOTANICAL NAME:
Magnolia

SOUNDS LIKE:
Magnolia

COMMON NAME:
Magnolia

TYPE:
Small to large, evergreen or deciduous, robust flowering tree; 12 to 40 feet

BASIC NEEDS:
Sun to part shade, adequate water, well-drained, humus-rich soil

WORST ENEMY:
Overwatering; flowering compromised by excessive shade

BEST ADVICE:
M. sieboldii is the easiest of the late-blooming magnolias to grow

Mid-seventeenth-century France was a lousy place for a young Protestant who wanted to go to college. Odds were good he (she? ha!) couldn't get in. Pierre Magnol must have been some kind of a guy to buck the system and become a brilliant professor of botany, so brilliant that his work inspired Our Father of the Plant Classification System, the eighteenth-century botanist Carl von Linné, a.k.a. Carolus Linnaeus.

Always one to acknowledge a colleague, Linnaeus paid great homage to Magnol. Today, few members of *Homo sapiens*—a Linnaean classification, by the way—who smell its fragrance or see its bloom do not know *Magnolia* by name.

Yet as widely planted as this genus is, a number of its superb species are missing from the landscape, particularly those that hold back bloom until the first spring orgy is over. At the top of the list is *M. sieboldii*, introduced more than a century ago from Japan. It's a small (twelve-feet), broad, shrubby magnolia with erect, egglike buds that open to firm, three- to four-inch cupped white blossoms, rich in fruity scent. The tree flowers from late May to July and has been known to toss on a few blooms in August. Even then, the show isn't over—not until the psychedelic-pink seedpods sing.

M. sieboldii has a lovely silvery silhouette, its candelabra shape evocative of welcoming arms opened wide. It's also the easiest of the late bloomers to grow, and the only one that can take full sun.

Afternoon shade is a must for the closely related *M. wilsonii*, which has much larger leaves (sometimes ten inches long) and similarly stunning, fragrant white flowers. The telling difference is that the Wilson magnolia's blossoms hang upside down (all the better to show their rose-crimson anthers), and therefore beg to be gazed up into. This is easily accomplished when the tree is planted on a slope or in a berm.

Both of these stunners will leave you wanting nothing, I mean nothing, for fragrance. But if you're a glutton for sensation (or have a weak sense of smell), a deep breath of *M. watsonii* (syn *M.* × *wiesneri*) is your fix. Its six-inch ivory flowers are positively overwhelming, borne on a twenty-foot tree with a heavier feel in the landscape that shows its best shape when pruned.

Last, a magnolia celebrated for its foliage rather than its flowers: *M. macrophylla*. Its many common names give a lot away about this American native that was grown by the Empress Josephine, certainly the first on *her* block to have a (choose one) bigleaf, great-leaved, elephant ear, big bloom, or cucumber tree.

We're talking about a huge (forty feet), fast-growing, and tropical-feeling shade tree with leaves the size of a five-year-old child. This species has a texture that will dominate a landscape; give it a comfy corner out of the wind so that its showy, three-foot leaves won't get tattered. Its fragrant, June/July flowers, fifteen inches across, are similarly outlandish, as are the mega seed cones that follow. Admittedly, both are slightly obscured high up among the plant's whorling, helicopter-blade leaves.

A postscript concerning Pierre Magnol: In all likelihood, the good professor never laid eyes on his namesake. The magnolia was introduced to Europe—and then only to a privileged few—a mere six years before his death.

gimme more

Here are two late-blooming, native evergreens:

M. grandiflora 'Edith Bogue':
Hardier, easier, and tidier than most of the big summer bloomers; 20 to 30 feet

M. virginiana (sweetbay magnolia):
Multistemmed, moisture-loving, and incredibly versatile. 'Henry Hicks' and 'Satellite' are more reliably evergreen selections; 10 to 15 feet in height and width.

Magnolia

Phlox

Its name comes from the Greek word for "flame," but forget that for a moment. Think instead of a dappled woodland garden in early spring.

Everything is stirring. Unfurling ferns rub their eyes, and sleek Solomon's seal is rising; ephemeral flowers make their oh-so-brief rendezvous with pollinators, while sweet young hostas are accosted by slugs.

Oops. Sorry. Take Two:

Sweet young hosta leaves tussle for daylight as the last of the lemony daffodils fade, and wave upon wave of blue woodland phlox *(Phlox divaricata)* roll by and drift away.

Now that's how I like my phlox—not screaming bloody murder like the moss phlox *(P. subulata)* that is already flowing like lava down innumerable city streets. I'm not saying moss phlox isn't a good, tough plant, I'm just saying some selections are quite overwhelming. On the other hand, even at its loudest, woodland phlox still lets you listen to the soft murmur of spring.

Consider the boldest of the bunch, introduced to the Northwest by Oregon Trail Gardens in Boring, Oregon: *P. stolonifera* 'Variegata'. Do not for a moment confuse it with that garish hussy of a summer garden phlox, *P. paniculata* 'Nora Leigh'. Instead, think of 'Variegata' as Nora's Cinderella sister, inherently beautiful without hitting you over the head. This rich pink creeping phlox spreads by runners that root along the ground, but you'll wish she *were* invasive. 'Variegata' is even less aggressive than the forms with dark green foliage, which can be planted at least a foot apart and won't take too long to fill the space.

P. stolonifera is an East Coast native that thrives in shade (light shade, that is; flowering will be sparse in deep shade) and looks good all year. It's represented in the trade by a number of white, mauve, and rich purple selections, all of which form

the facts

BOTANICAL NAME:
Phlox

SOUNDS LIKE:
Flocks

COMMON NAME:
Creeping phlox
(P. stolonifera); woodland
phlox (P. divaricata); moss
phlox (P. subulata)

TYPE:
Early-spring-blooming
perennial

BASIC NEEDS:
Part sun to light shade (not
full shade); rich, evenly
moist, well-drained soil

WORST ENEMY:
Drought

BEST ADVICE:
Plant in drifts, seas, waves—
anything but onesies

spring

44

prostrate mats of creeping stems with starry, open-faced flowers.

If *P. stolonifera* hugs, *P. divaricata* hovers. The blue woodland phlox is nearly twice as high (to the knee when in flower) and twice as sweet; its other name is wild sweet William. Plants will cover ground more slowly than *P. stolonifera*, but we're still talking a creeping mound.

P. stolonifera 'Variegata'

Though each of its petals is notched at the tip for a somewhat showier flower, what really undoes me about the long-blooming *P. divaricata* is what it makes of the color blue: icy, subtle, rich, or startling, depending on the selection. Out of flower, it doesn't have quite the foliage presence of *P. stolonifera* (it's not as dense a cover); its strength is not as a specimen but as a mingler, chatting its way across the woodland floor.

P. adsurgens '**Wagon Wheel**':
Salmon-flowered cultivar of a Siskiyou Mountain species; good drainage

P. divaricata cultivars:
'**Dirigo Ice**':
Ice blue
'**London Grove Blue**':
Deep blue
'**Eco Texas Purple**':
Dark purple, red-violet eye

P. stolonifera cultivars:
'**Sherwood Purple**':
Deep bluish purple
'**Bruce's White**':
Pure white, yellow eye
'**Blue Ridge**':
Soft blue

P. x *chattahoochee*
(syn *P. pilosa* '**Moody Blue**'):
Deep violet with red-purple eye

Phlox

4 5

Pleione

BULBOUS PLANT

Pleione

the facts

BOTANICAL NAME:
Pleione

SOUNDS LIKE:
Plea a knee

COMMON NAMES:
Windowsill orchid, Chinese
crocus orchid

TYPE:
Spring-blooming, exotic
woodland plant

BASIC NEEDS:
Part to full shade, well-
drained soil

WORST ENEMIES:
Drought, nasty drainage,
prolonged single-
digit temperatures

BEST ADVICE:
Start with five *P. formosana*
for a reasonable show

"Hardy orchids" sounds like an oxymoron. Come to think of it, they look sort of funny, too. Stare into just about any orchid long enough, and the view gets pretty weird. Take it from Susan Orlean, who gazed into hundreds of them while writing her book, *The Orchid Thief*:

"I kept seeing faces in the crinkles and spikes—little tongues, blind eyes, puffy lips, pugilists' squashed noses, a lobster, a caterpillar with a grin." And, in one spectacular instance, " . . . the face and silhouette of a poodle riding in a car with the windows open so its ears were blown back from its face."

I can't guarantee what you'll see if you go eye to eye with *Pleione*, but if you've got a cushy, well-drained woodland spot, chances are you'll get to do some gazing. This hardy orchid is neither finicky nor high-maintenance, yet it's still exotic and sublime.

Consider its life cycle. While dormant, it's a little green pseudo-bulb that sits turtle-like on the soil surface; come spring, it lifts its six-inch spike of a head, topped by at least one fat-lipped flower. As

the flower fades, leaves and roots begin to emerge (imagine the turtle growing legs and ears), with one single, pleated leaf staying the course.

By late summer, a new pseudobulb starts to form at the base of that leaf, and by late fall, the old pseudobulb withers away. Then you're back to dormancy, which on its own is quite the curiosity. You'll want to tuck the little greenback under a mulch comforter once the weather gets cold.

This is not your ordinary spring flower, with its whiskered, gaping maw (the lip), set in an airborne arrangement of straplike petals in colors ranging from pristine white to hot-pants pink. Given that the whole concoction doesn't reach more than six inches, ostentation is not a worry. In fact, one lone pleione will never do.

Even moisture through summer, protection from afternoon sun, and a spot preferably not under a large shade tree will work (the coarse, fallen foliage could smother them). Local pleione peddler Dick Cavender, owner of Red's Rhodies in Sherwood, Oregon, has had better luck growing his various gems under conifers, in full shade and humusy soil.

As far as species go, if this is your first hardy orchid, the choice is easy: *P. formosana,* which comes in quite a few cultivars, each with its own—however subtle—idiosyncratic markings. Of course, since one orchid lover's smiling caterpillar is another's windblown poodle, you might do well to view the pinups in Cavender's mail-order catalog before choosing your orchid's face.

Incidentally, one of the common names for pleione is "windowsill orchid," since it can be grown in a shallow pan in any north- or east-facing window. Opting to grow pleiones indoors certainly increases your choice of species, but if you tend toward neglence when it comes to houseplants, stick with the hardy guys.

P. bulbocodioides
'Yunnan':
Rose pink or bright magenta with red-purple spotted lip

P. forrestii:
Bright yellow with red lip markings; you'll pay big time for this one

P. formosana:
Easy and prolific; pale pink to dark-lavender-flushed pink
'Achievement':
Pale mauve pink with heavily blotched lip
'Blush Of Dawn':
Pale lavender
'Lilac Pearl':
Pale lavender with red lip markings; a new introduction
'Oriental Splendor':
Dark lavender; the most free flowering
'Polar Sun':
White with yellow lip markings

P. limprichtii:
Pink to rose magenta, heavily spotted with brick red

Polygonatum odoratum 'Variegatum'

BULBOUS PLANT

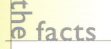

the facts

BOTANICAL NAME:
Polygonatum odoratum
'Variegatum'

SOUNDS LIKE:
A pig done ate 'em

COMMON NAME:
Solomon's seal

TYPE:
Spring blooming woodland
perennial

BASIC NEEDS:
Think hosta—bright shade,
moderately rich soil, good
drainage

WORST ENEMY:
Drought, slugs

BEST ADVICE:
If you've been reluctant to
try variegation in the garden, ease yourself in with
this classiest bicolored
beauty of all

I'll make this quick and to the point: If you've got a shade garden and can spare four square feet, buy five of the variegated Solomon's seal, *Polygonatum odoratum* 'Variegatum'. In a few years, you'll be evicting nearby squatters and spending more time on your hands and knees.

Here's a plant that draws you down to its level and makes you only wish you were that sublime. This woodland dweller is lit from within. Its airbrushed variegation works more like eyeliner than war paint, making its charm irresistible, even to those who generally shun foliage that thinks itself better than flowers.

Certainly, the leaves are the reason to grow this plant. Their airy, fine-boned grace is an enormous relief among densely textured hostas and multistained heuchera, and their stature gives weight to finely dissected dicentras and ground-hugging asarums. But the early spring flowers are far from subtle, particularly massed, when hundreds of creamy bells march two by two along the leaves.

P. odoratum 'Variegatum' (a.k.a. *P. odoratum* var. *thunbergii* 'Variegatum' and *P. falcatum* 'Variegatum') is, in fact, made for massing, and showy enough to hold its own in a mixed border (protected from afternoon sun under a small deciduous tree). I've also seen it leaping out of the dense shade beneath an American holly or leading visitors through lesser-traveled parts of the garden like lanterns along a path.

Clearly, this form is my favorite among the genus, but a number of others work in equally versatile ways. For a dwarf groundcover, the species *P. humile* rarely exceeds nine inches, small enough to occupy a swath of shade in the rock garden, where it will offer intrigue as soon as its spears break ground. The East Coast native Solomon's seal, *P. biflorum*, breaks like a wave in a woodland setting, arched over creeping phlox, sweet woodruff, or sheets of moss. It generally tops out at three feet and is not particularly aggressive, leaving ample room for fall bloomers to obscure its dying leaves.

gimme more

P. multiflorum x *P. odoratum* hybrids:
'Flore Pleno':
   Double-flowered
'Striatum':
   Also variegated, but less stunning than *P. odoratum* *'Variegatum'*

P. odoratum 'Variegatum'

If you're looking to fill space, consider the colonizing giant Solomon's seal *(P. commutatum)*, which emerges a deceptively fragile and thin-skinned pale gray-green. It's a great moist-edge-of-woodlands kind of plant that tends to gobble up the competition, making a sea of wafting, waving foliage often five to six feet high.

No biblical association accounts for why polygonatum is called Solomon's seal, but I have unearthed a couple of explanations. In the category Least Likely to Be True, it's said that when you cut into a polygonatum rhizome, the cross section looks like a six-pointed Star of David. Another theory dates from the late-sixteenth-century *Herball* of John Gerard, who praises the root's ability to seal broken bones ". . . gotten by falls or women's willfulness, in stumbling upon their hasty husbands' fists." (Wretched wenches, always in the way.)

But the most popular explanation is that the scars on the plant's rhizome—left by old leaf stems—resemble an official wax seal. Only those with Solomon's wisdom know why it bears his name.

Polygonatum odoratum 'Variegatum'

49

Primula

WOODLAND PERENNIAL

Four centuries ago, garden writer Agostine del Riccio sat chewing on the end of his quill, thinking up a flower garden good enough for an Italian king. "I know," he said to no one in particular. "What about those yellow jobs over at the Medici palazzo? Primroses!"

This plant has been around.

I used to hate primroses. Until I realized that only one kind was the source of my scorn: those congested, crinkle-leaved plants with their hideous neon flowers, the ones you see self-destructing in sidewalk containers and sold outside supermarkets by the pound.

Know the plants?

But it turns out there's a mind-boggling assortment of primroses that bear no resemblance to their mass-marketed cousins. Growers are now offering a range of species and cultivars that run the gamut from subtle to jaw-drop stunning.

Primula veris, known as cowslip, is much beloved in its native British Isles, where it naturalizes in meadows. In the Northwest, it likes a bit of shade, all the better to show off its nodding, butter-yellow flowers. It's a prolific bloomer, fragrant and, best of all, easy to grow.

Primula sieboldii, the Siebold prim-rose, is hands-down one of prettiest in the family, with flowers like those of woodland phlox in white through rose and lavender. It's also one of the best

P. veris

P. vialii

the facts

BOTANICAL NAME:
Primula

SOUNDS LIKE:
Fibula

COMMON NAME:
Primrose

TYPE:
Spring-blooming perennial

BASIC NEEDS:
Light shade, even moisture, well-drained, amended soil

WORST ENEMY:
Slugs, root weevils, summer drought

BEST ADVICE:
Resist the standard fare and experiment; start with the candelabra hybrids if you've got a soggy spot with some sun

spring

50

P. beesiana

primroses for a dry summer, as it goes dormant after flowering, thereby escaping the heat and drought that do in other
primulas. Two cultivars in particular are worth hunting
down: 'Yubisugata' with rich lavender petals underlined in
white, and the large-blossomed, aging to violet 'Blue'.

If you've got a soggy spot in the garden, go straight for
the candelabras, particularly the species that start with
"b": *P. beesiana, P. bulleyana,* and *P.* × *bullesiana* come in
June-bloom shades of peach, plum, and buttery yellow
on spikes up to three feet high. Consider placing them at
the bottom of a sloping lawn where it's often wet, or by a
pond if you've got one. You might even dig them their
own sweet bog.

But if tasteful's too tame for you, check out
Primula vialii, the so-called red-hot poker
primrose, a two-tone job that combines
lilac flowers with scarlet buds. It's
short-lived and will sulk and die if it dries
out, but it's worth the effort. Planted in a
mass, it's the last word in primroses.

P. sieboldii

**P. japonica 'Miller's
  Crimson':**
  Good red that seeds
  nicely

P. 'Linda Pope':
  A whopping 4-inch
  beauty with silver-edged
  foliage and mauve-blue
  flowers

Primula

5 1

Rosa glauca

DECIDUOUS SHRUB

the facts

BOTANICAL NAME:
Rosa glauca

SOUNDS LIKE:
How's about a

COMMON NAME:
Red-leaved rose (but
don't be fooled)

TYPE:
Upright, arching, multi-
stemmed rose with excep-
tional foliage; 6 to 8 feet

BASIC NEEDS:
Sun to part shade; drought-
tolerant once established

BEST ADVICE:
Pruning's a snap: keep the
plant simple, tall, and arching, and cut out old canes

A rose may be a rose, but add blue foliage and this rose confounds its genus. So atypical is the blue-leaved *Rosa glauca* that it unites two famously warring factions, gardeners who mollycoddle roses and those who spare no canes.

Being guilty of hacking many a hybrid tea, I have abiding faith in this upright and arching multistemmed shrub which—even without flowers—smells just as sweet (okay, I'll knock it off). Suffering from none of the narcissism of other roses, it does not devour attention but happily adapts to the role it's given. With its strong shape and the sense of motion that comes from its tumbling, poised-in-midair habit, *R. glauca* works as a hedge, in a mixed shrub border, or as a specimen among perennials.

This dusty rose is simply unequaled in its genus for foliage, whether it appears bluish gray in full sun, with shimmering over-tones of burgundy and mauve, or with an icing of silvery gray-green in part shade. Its color, like its habit, is a pleasure to work with, since it enhances everything that grows near it. I've admired it mixed with the moody purple leaves of smokebush *(Cotinus)*, the airy lavender flowers of meadow rue *(Thalictrum)*, and the steely blue spikes of blue oat grass *(Helictotrichon)*. Perhaps you have a golden groundcover that might glow brighter in blue-leaved shade.

R. glauca flowers a clear (albeit almost scentless) pink, with a white center studded by prominent yellow stamens. These blossoms are simple, single, and open-faced: less than two inches across and held in small flat clusters along the plant's arching frame, they seem to surf their way from branch to branch. In late summer, the flow-ers give way to bunches of orange rose hips that quickly fade to brownish-red, not prominent enough to scream out from a distance (for that you need *R. rugosa*), but a welcome ornament all the same.

The descendant of *R. canina*, the ancient dog rose, *R. glauca* was introduced prior to the 1830s, yet surprisingly to my knowledge there are no cultivars in the trade. I know absolutely nothing about hybridizing — perhaps, as with the Montagues and Capulets, there are political reasons why this species doesn't mix with others — but a white-flowered *R. glauca* would seem just the thing on a hot, thirsty day.

R. glauca

Sambucus

DECIDUOUS SHRUB

BOTANICAL NAME:
Sambucus

SOUNDS LIKE:
Can't nuke us

COMMON NAME:
Elderberry

TYPE:
Tall, wide, dense, deciduous
shrub, 5 to 15 feet

BASIC NEEDS:
Average in every way

WORST ENEMY:
Excessive shade

BEST ADVICE:
Keep shrub to a few
upright, open, and arching
stems for a glorious specimen, or whack stems back
in late winter for a modest
4- to 6-foot plant

Tired of reading about extraordinary plants you won't be able to grow because everything you bring home from the nursery just shrivels, sulks, and dies? Well, if you promise not to put them in a dark corner with wretched soil and deprive them of light and water, I'd like to turn you on to a few fabulous shrubs you will not be able to kill.

I hope.

The genus *Sambucus,* or elderberry, has the unenviable reputation of being a coarse, lanky, and out-of-control shrub. "If you have a small garden," one of my reference books says, "there is no reason for you to read about elders." (And people think *I* have an attitude.) Admittedly, our native, thicket-forming American elderberry, *Sambucus canadensis,* is not one to tuck in among your perennials, but so what. If there's a wild area in your garden and you do the edible plant thing, make this your first stop for elderberry jam, jelly, and wine.

Since my shtick is foliage, that's what I'm pushing. I've got two purples, going once, going twice, sold! to *S. nigra* 'Guincho Purple', whose dark green leaves mature to sumptuous black-purple (and hold through summer), then turn spirited red in fall. Old G. P. seems to be eclipsing *S. nigra* 'Purpurea', whose leaves are more likely to fade (though if you're in the Southeast, even G. P. goes a sweaty green). Nevertheless, 'Purpurea' is a stunner in spring: by the time the flower buds plump up, the shrub has reached its deepest hue, all the better to set off its creamy pink blooms.

Sambucus

S. nigra cultivars:
'Pulverulenta':
    Beautiful, plentiful
    white variegation on an
    extremely, and I mean
    extremely, slow-growing
    shrub; part shade,
    4 to 6 feet
'Variegata':
    Showy, robust, whack-
    backable large shrub or
    small tree

S. racemosa 'Sutherland Gold' offers sunlight bright-ness that never fades. Its finely dissected foliage emerges bright gold and remains audacious all season — particularly in summer, when it dolls itself up in translu-cent, scarlet fruit. This relatively recent Canadian hybrid does not burn in full sun, unlike the century-old favorite, *S. racemosa* 'Plumosa Aurea'. The latter red-berried elder, still championed by a few as the best gold-leaved shrub in cultivation, is slower growing and absolutely needs part shade.

S. nigra 'Laciniata', the fern-leaved elder, commands attention with texture rather than color; its tropically bold, deeply divided foliage makes it a valuable foil for generic greenery. A robust grower with big, white, flat June flowers, 'Laciniata' offers quite an impact without taking up too much visual space, and can double nicely as a jungle gym for flowering vines.

S. nigra 'Madonna' is a hot little number that also associates well with vines—or with any smaller plants that can make the most of her bright yellow variegation. Renowned for her diminutive stature—roughly four feet at maturity—she's one elderberry that doesn't tax your skills at managing size and scale. The only draw-back is that 'Madonna' is a tad harder to please, which may increase the likelihood that you will kill her. And we don't want that.

Or do we? The late, great horticulturist, J. C. Raulston once said, "You're not stretching yourself as a gardener if you're not killing plants." See what good gardeners we are?

Sanguinaria canadensis

BULBOUS PLANT

S. canadensis

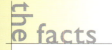

the facts

BOTANICAL NAME:
Sanguinaria canadensis

SOUNDS LIKE:
Sanguine area ban a dentist

COMMON NAME:
Bloodroot

TYPE:
Spring-blooming perennial

BASIC NEEDS:
Part to full shade; evenly
moist, rich, well-drained soil

WORST ENEMY:
Bloodroot is toxic; don't
ingest any part of the plant

BEST ADVICE:
Hide these gems like
Easter eggs throughout
the woodland

If plants could talk . . .

Frankly, I hadn't given the subject much thought until I started reading about the native East Coast bloodroot and thinking about the parade of humanity it has seen.

Who knows how many thousands of years passed in the forests of Pennsylvania before *Sanguinaria canadensis* observed its first human face? Whose face was it? Maybe it was that of a little Shawnee boy running barefoot through the woods, unaware that the face paint he couldn't wait to wear came from the blood-red roots of the plants underfoot.

Perhaps the day before, or a century later, it was the face of an elderly Cherokee woman in the forests of North Carolina, gathering those same plants for a decoction to quiet her husband's cough.

What else has *S. canadensis* seen? The Massachusetts woods crawling with men in white wigs and red coats, carrying muskets instead of baskets; the hills of Virginia, where men in blue and gray uniforms destroyed each other and the forest floor.

Then came the road crews with their Porta-Pottys and front-end loaders, the plant poachers who dug up woodland dwellers by the ton. Pity the downtrodden bloodroots! Do we even want to hear what they might say?

With any luck, it might be this: "All is forgiven." Because despite its modest size, tenderly rounded leaves, and easily shattered flowers, *S. canadensis* has survived it all—in our gardens if not in the wild. Besides, there's been plenty of good in those human faces. Witness the wonder expressed by Mrs. William Starr Dana, walking the woods of upstate New York a century ago:

"In early April, the curled-up leaf of the bloodroot, wrapped in its paper bracts, pushes its firm tip through the earth and brown leaves, bearing within its carefully shielded burden, the young erect flower-bud. When the perils of the way are passed and a safe height is reached, this pale, deeply lobed leaf resigns its precious charge and gradually unfolds itself; meanwhile the bud slowly swells into a blossom."

The flower of *S. canadensis* is, without a doubt, a particularly precious charge, each pristine white blossom the work of up to a dozen straplike petals surrounding a ray of bright yellow stamens. But it's not just its satiny sweetness that makes the bloodroot flower so irresistible: it's also its ephemeral nature. Breathe too heavily and the petals shatter, the moment gone.

The good news is that this member of the poppy family will self-sow to form larger, more satisfying colonies each year (besides, the wonderfully lobed foliage is more than half the plant's charm). The even better news is the cultivar 'Multiplex' (syn. 'Flore Pleno'), a drop-dead-gorgeous double-flowered form with twice the staying power and four times the number of petals (now imagine its price).

'Multiplex' is sterile, though, so to get more for your money you'll need to divide its rootstock when the leaves go dormant in fall. Cut into the juicy red rhizome—think war paint, cough syrup, love charm, even a plaque-inhibiting agent in toothpaste—and watch the lifeblood of human history flow.

Sanguinaria canadensis

Scrophularia auriculata 'Variegata'

PERENNIAL

the facts

BOTANICAL NAME:
Scrophularia auriculata
'Variegata'

SOUNDS LIKE:
Cough your area

COMMON NAME:
Water figwort

TYPE:
Showy-leaved, late-spring-
blooming perennial

BASIC NEEDS:
Sun to part shade;
damp soil

WORST ENEMY:
Drought

BEST ADVICE:
If you haven't deduced it
already, the key is to
give it wet feet

I really want you to remember this plant, but I'm not sure its history is the reason why. My dilemma concerns indelicacy, hard to avoid in the case of figwort, whose healing properties made it, in the Middle Ages, the darling of beleaguered hemorrhoid sufferers.

And that was only its secondary claim to fame. Its first had to do with "the King's evil"—the tubercular disease scrofula—the supposed cure of which earned this genus its decidedly unromantic name.

So is this a good time to tell you about *Scrophularia*'s cordovan-brown flowers, which a fellow garden writer likened to "rodent's eyes"?

Ah, but it's all uphill from here. *S. auriculata* 'Varie-gata'—a bicolored form of dubious medicinal value—is one of the choicest variegated-foliage plants the perennial world has to offer. Extremely bright and full of optimism, with conspicuously large and crinkled leaves, it has a rigid upright habit that makes it a beacon in the garden, irresistible to all who visit.

A member of the family *Scrophulariaceae,* related to monkey flower, snapdragon, and penstemon, the variegated water fig-wort is not actually aquatic, but it's happiest with damp toes. It then stands about three feet high, dressed in scrumptious, showy leaves, each painted with an irregular apple-green island floating in a broad vanilla sea. Its vertical stems are ridged and squared. Its flowers tower another foot above the plant, beady-eyed, maybe, but still oddball and amusing, if only second best to the foliage.

S. auriculata 'Variegata' is a real shot in the arm among peren-nials and does wonders to enliven a monochromatic planting of medium-sized shrubs. Culturally, it's pretty straightforward, provided you've got soaker hoses or drip irrigation to keep it from drying out. Not that drought will kill it—this is one tough scroph—but what could be lush will begin to look starved, and its rich vanilla edges will scorch.

If you happen to suffer a severe need for variegation, consider this plant the poor man's *Symphytum × uplandicum* 'Variegatum'. The figwort is infinitely more available and far less expensive than the variegated Russian comfrey and provides a comparable (if less prestigious) cure.

S. auriculata 'Variegata'

Smyrnium perfoliatum

PERENNIAL

the facts

BOTANICAL NAME:
Smyrnium perfoliatum

SOUNDS LIKE:
Bernie numb,
her goalie ate 'em

COMMON NAME:
Perfoliate Alexander

TYPE:
Late-spring-blooming
perennial

BASIC NEEDS:
Sun to part shade, some
moisture, good drainage

WORST ENEMY:
That which protects
it, summer dormancy;
chances are good you'll
forget where this plant was
and slice/stomp/dump
it by mistake

BEST ADVICE:
Sprinkle seeds
around garden

I am nuts about plants with perfoliate leaves. Yes, I am a very cheap date.

"Perfoliate" describes leaves that seem to encircle a stem, such as the dusty blue discs on dried eucalyptus. Their stem arrangement reminds me of a magician's act with spinning saucers, each stacked on top of the other, all whirling furiously around what seems a single thin pole.

Perfoliated plants give the same visual illusion—a rigid line passing through a solid object. In fact, the solid objects in question—the leaves—simply grow around and clasp the stem.

Isn't that the greatest?

No? Well, perhaps I could interest you in a lime-green flower. I venture to say that "chartreusity" is even trendier these days than purple foliage, so combine that color with the subtle magic of perfoliation, and you'll see why *Smyrnium perfoliatum* is indeed a wondrous thing.

First, though, consider the name, too cute for words (Smurf alert). It's circuitously derived from "myrrh"—Greek for "perfume"—a reference to the plant's spicy-smelling roots. (The better-known species *S. olusatrum* is the herb black lovage.)

Then there are the chartreuse bracts, the plant's true ornamentation. As with plants such as poinsettia, it's the infertile bracts and not the fertile flowers that steal the show. In the case of smyrnium's showy bracts, the added bonus is that they are the perfoliate part! (What, you're not excited?) The actual leaves are just ordinary, celery-like jobs; the bracts are the source of the magic.

Annual, biennial, triennial? "Yes," says Marietta O'Byrne of Northwest Garden Nursery, one of the first U.S. propagators of *S. perfoliatum*. "We planted seeds last year. They came up, then disappeared in summer. They're up again now but they won't flower till next year, so I consider them triennial."

The *S. perfoliatum* sold in her nursery will bloom in its third year, but because the plant's monocarpic, it will die. Not to worry. Gardeners can let plants reseed in place, or widen their sphere of influence by sprinkling seed throughout the garden.

O'Byrne grows *S. perfoliatum* with more visible companion plants that will protect it during summer dormancy from a rude (read: overzealous gardener) awakening. One of her more stunning combos is with the emerging bronze foliage of the perennial *Cryptotaenia* and the saturated colors of June-blooming Asiatic lilies.

"But the reason I first hunted this plant down," she adds, "was the way it looked with red. I saw a photo of it combined with tulips in *Christopher Lloyd's Flower Garden* and said to myself, 'I gotta have this plant.'" Looks like she's a pretty cheap date, too.

S. perfoliatum

Smyrnium perfoliatum

Tiarella

the facts

BOTANICAL NAME:
Tiarella

SOUNDS LIKE:
Me 'n' Della

COMMON NAME:
Foamflower

TYPE:
Spring-blooming, woodland
semi-evergreen perennial

BASIC NEEDS:
Part to full shade, good
drainage, rich, evenly
moist soil

WORST ENEMY:
Drought

BEST ADVICE:
Plant in drifts

Long ago and far away—at least seven years in hybridist time—the genus *Tiarella*, or foamflower, was an easy one to master. The choices were simple: runner or clumper? If you wanted a runner, you bought *T. cordifolia;* the clumper was *T. wherryi* (syn. *T. cordifolia* var. *collina*). If you grew *Tiarella* 'Oakleaf' (or even more so, 'Slickrock'), you were clearly connected to the *sanctum sanctorum* of native-plant nerds.

Then along came three talented (and insatiable) propagators: Sinclair Adam Jr. of Dunvegan wholesale nursery in Coatesville, Pennsylvania, Don Jacobs of Eco-Gardens in Decatur, Georgia, and Dan Heims of Terra Nova Nurseries in Canby, Oregon. By the time they were finished (please, God, are they finished yet?), nature's tiarellas looked like mere chocolate pudding compared with all this manmade chocolate mousse.

Are we happy? Sure. Are we confused and overwhelmed? You bet.

It was with great difficulty that we singled out one cultivar for illustration, but the leaves of 'Cygnet' are a fair sampling of tiarella foliage at its best: deeply, I mean deeply, divided, with one prominent lobe and a near-black central blotch that pulls the eye straight in. "No ugly duckling here," writes the plant's hybridizer, Dan Heims, father to some dozen vainglorious forms. Several boast 'Cygnet's long-fingered leaves; others have more intricate blotching. (Heims wanted to call one of them 'Rorschach' but settled on 'Inkblot'.)

But maybe I've jumped the gun here. Why should you grow tiarella? Perhaps because it's one of the most satisfying four-season woodland plants you'll ever have the pleasure of knowing. My selections of this *Saxifrage* family genus are bronze and beautiful through the winter, their soft furry leaves cuddled together in enviably snug mounds. By mid-March, they are awake and upwardly mobile, soft pink buds riding tall rosy stems, a kid's-drawing version of an evergreen (skinny trunk with a triangle up top).

Midspring is the time for the flowers, whose primary charm is their overall foamy effect (hence the common name, foam-flower). Since the more foam, the more intoxicating the bubbles, you'll be pleased to know that a four-inch pot burgeons quickly into a foot-wide, giddy groundcover, punctuated by dense spikes of soft white to cloudy-pink blooms. It's a lovely sight that soon becomes remarkable for one good reason: Once a tiarella is in flower, it never seems to stop.

T. 'Cygnet'

So, back to the selections. Prepare yourself for a provocative assortment of Heimsian names, such as 'Mint Chocolate' (mint-green leaves with a dark over-lay), 'Skeleton Key' (with cut leaves that rival those of 'Cygnet') and the beautifully flow-ered 'Spring Symphony'. You may also come across other hybridizers' handiwork, including plants with the prefix 'Eco' (from Don Jacobs's Eco-Gardens). But if you believe that Ma Nature does it best, look for the might-ily spreading 'Slickrock', no longer the darling of the in-crowd but a reassuring reminder of simpler times.

Tiarella

Zenobia pulverulenta

DECIDUOUS SHRUB

the facts

Ode to a Queen:

Zenobia, Queen of Palmyra, A.D. 266! Did your skin glow pale in the moonlight? Were your robes made of opals and pearls? Is your sister Priscilla, Queen of the Desert? Whoops. I digress.

Zenobia! Last in all shrub literature, first in my heart. Good to see you so widely planted in the Northwest. Took a while, I know, but what a pleasure you've finally arrived.

Was it your foliage that finally brought the gardening world to its senses? I can well see why. In my own garden, short of *Mertensia asiatica*—which remains a dicey proposition—nothing holds a candle to your white-washed blue. I hope you don't mind that I show everyone who visits the impossibly glaucous undersides of your leaves; it's just that I don't think they'd believe me if I simply said "They're as ghostly as the ocean when the moon turns it silver and still."

And your new growth! How do you manage to achieve that faint raspberry stain on your minuscule young leaves? It's a fleeting touch and a marvel of the moment, which stays with me (if not you) all season, so that I always think of you as blushing just the slightest violet red.

Zenobia! I admire your tenacity. I've seen you clutch your foliage to your quaking stems through howling, winter winds. I admit you can be a little too greedy, wanting to hold on to what's past when it's time to let go, so I hope you don't mind that I sometimes give your winter-worn leaves a little tug.

No, I haven't forgotten your flowers, carillons of pure white, fragrant bells which, in your wisdom, you display from the tips of your cinnamon-brown branches. Such simple elegance! Such class! I love their music, their precision, their perseverance. And I can tell you enjoy your baubles—your proud, arching habit seems ever so slightly enhanced when your fingertips sparkle.

How tall can you make yourself? Three feet? Five feet? I await your full splendor. I hope you like where I've put you, with not-so-nearly-blue sedum, a raven-winged *Anthriscus*, and a lovely blueberry who so resembles you. Or, if you prefer, I can procure that gorgeous blue *Cerinthe* whose purple flowers will make you blush, and lay a richly brocaded burgundy *Heuchera* at your feet should you grow cold.

Zenobia! I will never desert you. But beware of pretenders to your throne. There are many far less blue, and though rightful heirs to your genus, they go positively green beside the resplendent, dusty you.

Z. pulverulenta

summer

Angelica gigas

BIENNIAL

the facts

BOTANICAL NAME:
Angelica gigas

SOUNDS LIKE:
I'm telling ya ghee guss

COMMON NAME:
Purple-flowered wild
parsnip

TYPE:
Summer-blooming biennial

BASIC NEEDS:
Full sun to light shade,
ample moisture, rich soil

WORST ENEMY:
Slugs, nasty soil, drought

BEST ADVICE:
First year is critical: Keep
well watered, fertilize, and
squash those slugs

If Euell Gibbons had gone stalking the wild parsnip instead of the wild asparagus—in particular, the purple-flowered species, *Angelica gigas*—the result would have been a lurid thriller rather than his tame tome on wild food.

This plant is so sexy, describing its parts is embarrassing.

Inflated, purple-veined leaf sheaths; broad-fingered, massive leaves; dark, swollen buds opening to densely packed, five-inch flower heads of black-purple brocade. All this might have gone unnoticed had *A. gigas* been humble in size. But no, it insists on flexing its five- to six-foot presence with a foliage span three feet wide.

Long used by the Chinese American community as a medicinal herb, *A. gigas* was first introduced to the U.S. as a garden plant in the late 1970s by plantsman Barry Yinger, proprietor of Asiatica, in Lewisberry, Pennsylvania. Yinger was no doubt completely taken aback when he saw these lurid purple giants (his words) growing wild in Korean ravines. Even now, *A. gigas* seems impossible, such architectural audacity combined with a summer color hinted at by eggplant and confirmed by dark cherries and burgundy grapes.

But there it is: an easily grown, sun-to-part-shade, moisture-loving biennial that—like hollyhock—flowers from seed in two years, then duplicates itself if you're lucky (or costs a few bucks to replace if you're not).

A member of the family *Umbelliferae*, which also includes carrots and fennel, the genus *Angelica* is more popularly represented by the ordinary wild parsnip, *A. archangelica* (syn. *A. officinalis*). This herb possesses striking, tropical leaves similar to those of *A. gigas* and can get seven feet high, but is nothing to shout about when in flower. It's more utilitarian than ornamental, with edible leaves and stalks, and roots that are used in flavoring liqueurs.

By no means a slouch, the so-called garden angelica makes a substantial presence in a natural setting, particularly streamside. But in the average urban garden, where space is at a premium and plants need to perform, it seems a waste to pass up something seriously naughty and settle for simply nice. Unless, that is, you are after seriously naughtier: *A. stricta* 'Purpurea.' Check out this hearbreakingly sumptuous purple-leaved, purple-flowered form.

A. gigas

Buddleia

SEMI-EVERGREEN SHRUB

If it's purple, and it's summer, it's *Buddleia*. The butterfly bush is fast becoming America's favorite hot-weather shrub. Cultivars of *B. davidii* are remarkably fast growing and quick to flower, in goose-neck panicles of indigo, lavender, pink, and white. Slice them, dice them, prune the bejeezus out of them, and they come back laughing for more.

Little can be done to discourage the butterfly bush, but just because it insists on growing doesn't mean you've grown it well. Without full sun it gets weedy, and without annual pruning— preferably down to a foot—it looks stretched and sparse.

Though ubiquitous, these summer lilacs are simply too valuable for even plant snobs to dismiss. Instead, we like to carry on about the species nobody knows. *B. globosa* has been in cultivation for two hundred years, but is only just hitting the U.S. mail-order market. Unfortunately, its common name takes all the mystery out of the romance: the orange ball tree. Yep, that pretty much sums it up.

The globed flowers, less than an inch in diameter, range from Aspergum orange to lemon yellow and pop like bingo balls off the plant. The leaves are long, dark, and wrinkled, with white, felted backs, and are much less coarse than those of *B. davidii*. It is also slightly less hardy (it's native to Peru and Chile), but is similar in size and has an infinitely better sense of humor.

Like parent, like child: *B. × weyeriana* has a similarly sunny dis-position, particularly the glowing orange cultivar, 'Sungold'. This time the flower globes are in more tightly packed terminal panicles, a sort of cross between the orange ball tree and the common butter-fly bush (which is precisely what this species is). Other hybridized benefits: 'Sungold' is hardier than *B. globosa* and flowers over a longer period of time.

Because both globular species flower on old wood, you don't prune them until after they've flowered. The same holds true for the fountain buddleia, *B. alternifolia*, another species whose essence is captured by its common name. With a habit like a miniature weeping willow, this fragrant, lilac-pink buddleia is unlike any of the others because it blooms along the arms of its branches rather than off the branch ends. The effect is pretty spectacular in June, and the shrub's not half bad after flowering; some gardeners even train it into a fountainesque small tree.

If you can find the *B. alternifolia* cultivar 'Argentea', you'll get an even better foliage effect from its season-long, silvery gray leaves. Or, if you've evolved beyond the need for opulent, perfumed blooms, you can try the arresting, lamb's ear–foliaged *B. nivea*. But if you're resolute in your need for big old butterfly flowers in some near-shade of purple, I vote for the well-shaped *Buddleia* 'Lochinch', credited to Scotland's Earl of Stair. It has downy young stems, leaves undercoated with white felt, and lilac-blue flowers with laughing orange eyes.

B. globosa

Clethra

DECIDUOUS SHRUB

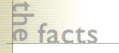

the facts

C. alnifolia

BOTANICAL NAME:
Clethra

SOUNDS LIKE:
Plethora

COMMON NAME:
Summersweet, sweet
pepperbush

TYPE:
Thicket-forming summer-
blooming deciduous shrub;
4 to 8 feet

BASIC NEEDS:
Air and water; so tough it
can take shade and flooding

WORST ENEMY:
Drought

BEST ADVICE:
Leave the spent seedpods
as winter ornaments, then
tip back the branches (or
cut older stems to the
ground) in early spring

Clethra alnifolia is a hard-working, sweet-natured shrub. She's the kind of make-the-best-of-it, low-maintenance being I fear I'll never be. She can take a tough situation—for example, a gloomy, damp day—throw down the ground cloth and the blanket, and unpack a picnic with enough surprises to chase away all deprivation.

Nicknamed summersweet in her hometown of East Coast, USA, Clethra thrives on moisture. Overindulges, if the truth be known. With nothing nearby to check her growth, she can expand indefinitely (via colonizing suckers), yet nobody seems to much mind. The reason: Her intensely fragrant midsummer flowers, which come at a time when competition is at a lull. These clusters of white bottlebrush blossoms smother her upright-to-rounded body and beckon passersby like a siren's song. Rumor has it that in the days when Ahab commanded the *Pequod*, she was known as sailor's delight. Seems her delicious smell wafted o'er the waters and reached returning whalers even before the guy in the crow's nest spied land.

Outside of her native haunts, though, *C. alnifolia* can be a bit plain (some say coarse), particularly when asked to hold her own in a more polished urban garden. Fortunately, she's got some citified cousins with extremely desirable charms: petite stature ('Hummingbird', with forms varying from eighteen inches to four feet); pastel color ('Pink Spires' and 'Rosea'); richer hue ('Fern Valley Pink' and 'Ruby Spice'); and my favorite, speckled leaves ('Creel's Calico'). Though all these cultivars thrive on ample water, they're just fine in ordinary soil and are easily integrated into mixed borders, where it's simple to contain their spread with a sharp spade.

Siting, however, is crucial, because clethra's sweet flowers are magnets for bees. Not a great choice near a seating area, but just fine near a bedroom window—assuming you have screens. The shrubs are extremely floriferous, the blossoms are long lasting, and the spent seed heads look great through the winter, like peppercorn beads on a string (hence summersweet's other nickname, sweet pepperbush).

With all due respect to summersweet's charms, you need to know about her gorgeous Asian cousin, *C. barbinervis*, who makes the picnic laid out by *C. alnifolia* look like a wet blanket heaped with fodder. This epicurean, statuesque shrub/small tree has a candelabra-like branching habit and twenty-foot limbs of enormous grace. Its striking leaf canopy shows off its peeling, polished trunk, which nearly (but not quite) rivals that of *Stewartia*. This is a long-haul landscape plant, however, and needs to know you pretty well before it starts shedding bark. So if you're starved for sensation and can't commit, indulge in summersweet.

C. tomentosa (syn C. alnifolia var. tomentosa):
Woolly summersweet, later flowering, more heat tolerant form; felted stems and leaves with white undersides; native to coastal Southeast

C. fargesii:
Vigorous, upright, tiered shrub to 12 feet with up to 8-inch dangling white flowers; from China

C. pringlei:
Large textured foliage and lacy flowers on a narrow tree; no single-digit winters; from central Mexico

Clethra

Cotinus

DECIDUOUS SHRUB OR TREE

the facts

BOTANICAL NAME:
Cotinus

SOUNDS LIKE:
Your Highness

COMMON NAME:
Smokebush (*C. coggygria*),
smoke tree (*C. obovatus*)

TYPE:
Smokebush—tall, spreading
deciduous shrub, 10 to 15
feet; smoke tree—upright,
medium-sized tree with
rounded crown, to 30 feet

BASIC NEEDS:
Sun, good drainage

WORST ENEMY:
Wet feet

BEST ADVICE:
Smokebush doesn't take
standard pruning well; either
leave it ample room or cut it
back to 1 foot in fall

Remember the last time you went to a nursery to buy someone a plant? And how you stood around, bewildered, maybe even a little cranky, wondering what to buy?

Here's a hint: I've never seen anyone look at a purple-leaved *Cotinus coggygria* and remain apathetic. Just the other day, my esteemed partner—a "no thanks, no plants" kind of guy—stopped in front of a smokebush and stared in uncharacteristic awe at its glowing mass of sun singed, blood-black foliage. (Frankly, I was more in awe of his reaction. Dare I hope he's coming around?)

Among the best dark-leaved smokebush cultivars on the market are 'Royal Purple', 'Velvet Cloak', 'Notcutt's Variety', and 'Nordine Red'. No doubt newer varieties are being unloaded at the nursery even as I write. These plants can be grown either as large, multi-stemmed shrubs (on average, twelve feet tall and wide) with vast, buff-pink-to-purple puffs in summer, or as walloping foliage accents for color-hungry gardens.

Wallop is precisely what you do to get the best foliage color out of a purple-leaved smokebush. Early each spring, cut the shrub back to within a foot of the ground. The technique—called stooling—may seem drastic, but the payoff is nearly immediate: lush and large-leaved four-foot pillars of deep wine reds or chocolate purples, depending on the cultivar you buy.

Of course, if you do whack back the shrub, forget about the smoke. By removing the current season's woody growth, you've nuked the flowers (and therefore the silklike hairs on the spent floral plumes that give the plant its common name). For a smoking bush, just let it grow.

And, might I add, grow. The shrub resents pruning (as opposed to stooling) and will develop gangly, whiplike stems to spite you if you try to keep it small.

One of the smokiest *C. coggygria* cultivars is the green-leaved form

'Daydream', chosen for its heavy-headed, rounded flower panicles that hover like clouds above a compact, ten-foot shrub. 'Flame', a blue-green-leaved cotinus with characteristic paddle-shaped leaves, is favored for its particularly brilliant orange-red fall color.

For the best of both worlds— soft red leaves that darken with age and massive amounts of smoke—the current rage is the long-legged, twenty-foot hybrid 'Grace', whose purplish pink flower clusters measure more than a foot long.

Yet if I had the space and knew I was staying put, my first choice would be the green-leaved American smoketree, *C. obovatus*, both because of its majestic presence and the statement it makes in the fall: a dynamic conflagration of yellow, orange, peach, and red. Seems the foliage was in such demand as a source of dye during the Civil War that *C. obovatus* in the wild was almost lost. Certainly the summer plumes on this handsome hunk are not as showy as those of *C. coggygria*. But when the smoke clears, *C. obovatus* is completely glorious and capable of inspiring awe, even in a "no plants" kind of guy.

C. obovatus

Echinops

PERENNIAL

Hate us if you must, but the Portland, Oregon, area can accommodate both the most catholic of plant tastes and the blackest-thumbed gardeners. Whether we're talking rare species rhodies or roadside fireweed *(Epilobium)* or a gardener who works with ease or with extreme aggravation, life in Zone 8 is ludicrously benign.

However, that doesn't necessarily mean everything grows well. A vast array of plants prefer their winters seriously cold. Not since I lived in New England have I seen lilacs, delphinium, bee balm *(Monarda)*, and purple coneflower *(Echinacea)* so gloriously grown.

But what I miss most from the small-town gardens of Vermont and upstate New York is the globe thistle, *Echinops*, whose deep blue flowers played like staccato notes along the staff lines of whitewashed picket fences. Strident, metallic, and majestically architectural, this plant was one of the payoffs for surviving the kind of winter where your nose hairs iced up the instant you walked outside.

E. ritro is native to southern France and Spain (though my first guess would have been Siberia). It's an unlikely member of the daisy family, with neither petals, a central ray, nor a remotely love-me/love-me-not look. Instead, the globe thistle sports jagged, spiny

E. ritro

the facts

BOTANICAL NAME:
Echinops

SOUNDS LIKE:
Peck a hops

COMMON NAME:
Globe thistle

TYPE:
Summer-blooming
perennial, to 4 feet

BASIC NEEDS:
Full sun, good drainage,
water until established

WORST ENEMY:
Richly amended soil

BEST ADVICE:
For an extremely playful
effect, repeat it in a border

summer

leaves (softer to the touch than they appear) and tall stems lit with bristly bracted flowers. These are plants you literally don't want to stumble into, both because of their edginess and inebriating appeal to bees.

But in a perennial border or as a cut-and-dry flower, *E. ritro* has enormous, classic charm. It combines the humor of a fat-headed allium with the austerity of a steely blue sea holly *(Eryngium)*, its one- to two-inch spherical blossoms balancing up to four feet in the air. Bloom time begins midsummer, and plants stay ornamental until mowed to the ground (one Seattle garden designer zaps autumn's fading flowers with red spray paint. Go figure). Flower color plays variations on the theme of metallic blue; often, the colder the nights, the richer the color.

Full sun and soil that drains are all it takes to grow *E. ritro.* Don't bother with cushy amendments, which will makes plants lazy and lax. No doubt you'll fuss more over selecting a cultivar or species than you will over digging this thistle a home.

The common wisdom on drying plants is to cut flowers before they open and hang them by their stems to dry. A few saved echinops stalks will afford you warm memories of August as you watch the landscape shiver in temperatures that thrill roots, if not toes.

All these are game for below 0°F:

E. bannaticus:
Foliage hairier and more deeply divided than that of *E. ritro*

'Blue Glow':
Darker blue cultivar (sometimes listed as a cultivar of *E. ritro*)

E. exaltatus:
Russian globe thistle; tennis ball–sized silvery white flowers; 6 feet

E. ritro:
'Taplow Blue':
Brighter than the species
'Veitch's Blue':
European favorite, darkest of the steely blues

E. sphaerocephalus
'Arctic Glow':
Gray-green leaves, silvery white flowers, thick red stems; 3 to 5 feet

Fallopia

SHRUBBY PERENNIAL

the facts

BOTANICAL NAME:
Fallopia (syn. Polygonum)

SOUNDS LIKE:
(Same as the tube)

COMMON NAME:
Variegated Japanese
knotweed

TYPE:
Upright, shrubby, robust
perennial

BASIC NEEDS:
Part shade to sun; even
moisture

WORST ENEMY:
Its own bad self; this is a
notoriously invasive genus

BEST ADVICE:
Keep a wary eye on both
of these beauties

Sometimes I go looking for trouble. This time trouble found me. Its name is *Fallopia* (syn. *Polygonum*), and had I any idea of the controversy surrounding it, I might have backed away from profiling this genus.

But based on the Oh wow! factor—the only possible reaction to one's first encounter with *Fallopia* in its variegated forms—it never occurred to me to keep the news of *Fallopia* 'Devon's Cream' and *F. japonica* 'Variegata' (syn. *Polygonum cuspidatum* 'Variegata') to myself.

Who could blame me? We're talking about big, leafy perennials that are ornamental from day one, their foliage the main attraction. 'Devon's Cream' has pink stems and custard-colored young leaves that are soon stained raspberry red and mottled two-tone green. 'Variegata' is an equally exquisite confection, with arching sprays of dramatically white-splashed foliage that emerges electric peach in spring.

But because of the grossly invasive nature of this genus, no discussion of the two variegated forms is possible without raising hackles high. Never mind that the straight species of Japanese knotweed are treacherous beasts, capable of gorging on Roundup and bellying up to the bar for more. Sane people do not grow these plants. But when it comes to the variegated forms, folks take sides.

In the "nohow, noway, nofallopia" corner we have Northwest plantsman Dan Hinkley, who has sworn off the genus altogether—with the exception of the superior, clumping cultivar *F. japonica* 'Crimson Beauty' (syn. *Polygonum cuspidatum* 'Crimson Beauty'). Hinkley says fallopias not only are aggressive garden thugs but are taking their toll on our natural ecosystems, where they've become rampant weeds.

In the "gorgeous plant, gotta-have-it" corner we have horticultural heavyweights such as Holly Shimizu, director of the Lewis Gintner Botanical Garden in Charlottesville, Virginia, where visitors will see 'Variegata' set off by a backdrop of weeping yew. (Says Shimizu of 'Variegata': "I love it! High ratings!") Closer to home, Oregon horticulturist Dan Heims—one of the plant's leading U.S.

proponents—happily takes credit for introducing 'Devon's Cream' from England, and offers tissue-cultured 'Variegata' by the tens of thousands. After observing both selections in his garden and seeing no sign of middle-age spread, Heims has high confidence in the plants.

How could Heims, Shimizu, and Hinkley be talking about the same plant? Heims says they aren't. He explains that years back, a disastrous and spreading variegated fallopia was introduced into commerce by the North Carolina State University Arboretum (now the J. C. Raulston Arboretum). This rogue gave the plant its current infamous reputation—and may well be the form Hinkley knows. Heims says what he's been offering is one he acquired independently from Japan (where it's called 'Milk Boy'), a well-behaved, non-invasive form. (This, by the way, is the plant Shimizu grows.) As for the possibility of its commingling with the already rampant knotweed and aiding and abetting its invasion in the wild, Heims points out that his female-only, tissue-cultured 'Variegata' clones are sterile (bringing to mind the purple loosestrife, whose cultivars were once also thought sterile; it simply wasn't so).

Here I am, then, betwixt and between, loving these plants as Heims and Shimizu do, but taking Hinkley's point to heart. I am growing 'Devon's Cream' in an urban setting hemmed in by stone walls and sidewalks; I've also planted 'Variegata' in a client's garden (now calm down, Alice), because it's going to look killer in front of her humongous arborvitae hedge, and it doesn't revert to green as does 'Devon's Cream'.

As a compromise, however, I've kept Alice's 'Variegata' within the confines of a gallon container sunk into the ground—and we'll both remain vigilant should the time come to exile the specimen to a penal patio pot.

Fallopia

Firmiana simplex

DECIDUOUS TREE

They call it Tropicalismo. I call it farcical gizmo. Excuse my atti-
tude, but do you truly hanker after a garden where gaily dressed
calypso musicians play on tortoise backs while tourists sip rum-
drenched drinks out of excavated fruit?

I propose we call a love of bold leaves and bright colors precisely what it is: good taste. Whether cannas or bananas, elephant ears
or hardy palms, the result is a diversity of texture—a vital element
for successful garden design.

So instead of a landscape with a label, consider a textural giant
with a wonderfully exotic tale. *Firmiana simplex*—a hardy member
of the chocolate family—is said to be the exclusive haunt of the
fabled Chinese phoenix, a creature with a fowl's head, a human's
eye, a serpent's neck, a swallow's brow, and a tortoise's back (purely
coincidental, I assure you).

The first recorded appearance of this birdlike creature forged of
fire was in 2600 B.C. Since it's thought to alight only in times of peace
and prosperity, contemporary phoenix-watchers have not been able
to check this one off their life lists. Nevertheless, a phoenix in the
garden is worth who-knows-how-many in the bush, or so thought
Chinese scholars, who believed the bird a source of inspiration, and
therefore planted *F. simplex* outside their places of work.

Ample, more tangible reasons exist to grow this twenty- to thirty-
foot tree: fabulously smooth green bark with branches arranged in
accentuated whorls; foot-wide (and then some) maplelike leaves; two-
foot panicles of small, lightly fragrant flowers that arch up and out
from its branch ends; and the subsequent parade of miniature-parasol-
like fruits that give the tree its common name, Chinese parasol tree.

These four- to five-inch rosy-pink umbrellas are actually the wrinkled outer skins of the fruit, which separate and pull away from the
pea-sized black seeds inside and appear to hover above them. The
papery skin, which ages and dries to the color of light cinnamon, is

evidently a charmer in dried arrangements.

In her invaluable book, *The Year in Trees*, co-authored with the ever-missed plantsman J. C. Raulston, horticulturist Kim Tripp describes being transported by the raining fruit. "You can almost make out those long-gone Victorians, fanning themselves and twirling their parasols under a far-off tropical sun." She goes on to write that the tree's fall color can be a bright canary yellow. Seattle plantsman Arthur Lee Jacobson takes a less fanciful tack, describing the foliage as "an ugly mix of wet cardboard color and green in late fall." No doubt the weather will have the final word about autumn, but as a source of bold texture and enormous inspiration, *F. simplex*'s presence in the landscape will defy cliché.

F. simplex

Fuchsia

SEMI-EVERGREEN SHRUB

the facts

BOTANICAL NAME:
Fuchsia

SOUNDS LIKE:
Few shuh

COMMON NAME:
Fuchsia

TYPE:
Upright, arching, fabulously long-blooming deciduous shrub or perennial

BASIC NEEDS:
Air, water (and the latter sparingly)

WORST ENEMY:
Single-digit temperatures

BEST ADVICE:
Mulch heavily and site out of wind; wait for new spring growth before pruning; tip-prune to shape

Leonhard Fuchs was a German physician and botanist who put foxglove on the map in his not-so-best-selling treatise *De historia stirpium* (1542).

Fuchs had been dead at least a century when a French Catholic priest named Père Plumier stumbled on a very un-foxglove-looking shrub while plant hunting in what is now the Dominican Republic. I haven't a clue why its airy being and dangling flowers made Plumier think of Fuchs, but in 1703 the priest introduced his find as the genus *Fuchsia*.

I'd never had much time for Fuchs's namesake, thinking it a very silly plant (fat-bellied, ding-dong, parachuting nuns' caps are the images that come to mind). I hadn't imagined fuchsias capable of the grace and delicacy I've since discovered so many of them have.

F. 'Hawkshead'

Nor had I imagined the sheer excess in this genus: hybridizers have unleashed some eight thousand varieties! But relax, we won't go there. Instead, let's talk about the uncomplicated, single-flowered forms.

Among the more ubiquitous hardy fuchsias in the Northwest is the iridescent pink 'June Bride' (three feet by three feet), a carefree shrub that remains in flower long after many shrubs have lost their leaves. Extremely demure—all right, girly—in color, 'June Bride' may be way too sweet if you like your fuchsias sassy. But in the right context (say, nestled among limbed-up rhodies) it appears smothered in fireflies half the year.

F. magellanica var. *molinae* (also sold as *F. magellanica* 'Alba') is a similarly chaste though exceptionally robust selection (seven feet by seven feet), its sepals (the flying-nun part of the flower) white, the corolla beneath barely pink. 'Hawkshead' (four feet by four feet) is another discriminating cultivar, a quiet white whiff of a blossom softened with just a hint of green.

For sassy, start with 'Caledonia' (two feet by two and a half feet), its flowers long, liquid strands of cherry red. Then on to the bicolored firecracker *F. magellanica* 'Riccartonii' (four feet by four feet), at least as ubiquitous as 'June Bride', and a tough old thing that's grown in Ireland as a hedge. 'David' (three feet by three feet) is also quite sturdy, with very small leaves and flowers, a free-flowering cultivar in shades of purple and cerise. And at the opposite end of the subtlety scale is the four-foot, bicolored 'Senorita' (who some say is *F. magellanica* var. *gracilis* in drag); in the language of hummingbirds, this one means fast food.

Fuchsias for foliage? Glad you asked. *F. magellanica* 'Tricolor' (syn. 'Versicolor', three and a half feet by four feet), has a two-tone cream-and-olive leaf softened by a wash of pink, with slender red flowers riding at the ends of its arching stems. And for weigela-bright yellow, make mine *F. magellanica* 'Aurea', (three feet by three feet) with stems and veins that turn magenta in fall.

But if I had room for only one fuchsia, it would be the Mexican shrublet 'Isis' (eighteen inches to four feet), so breathlessly subtle with its bite-size foliage and flower, you'll want to site it up close to know it's there. An easy mingler among perennials with its strongly vertical, irregular shape, 'Isis' can flower in August and then again in December, with the tiniest imaginable sparks of fire on the bravest of all plants.

Geranium

PERENNIAL

Hardy geraniums are wholesome garden inhabitants. They are familiar and therefore soothing, their faces an open book; you just can't help wanting to trust the gardener who grows them.

They're also largely unambitious, by which I mean they do not want starring roles. Hardy geraniums are the extras without which towns would be deserted and parties would be duds. Whether pink, purple, or 'Johnson's Blue', they mingle without much introduction. Just put a drink in their hands and they'll find their own way through diverse, even hostile, crowds.

I keep calling them "hardy geraniums" for those inclined to confuse these perennials with those fuzzy-leaved and floriferous red, pink, or white annuals, pelargoniums, that bloom in summer window boxes coast to coast.

The selection of hardy geraniums these days is nothing less than awesome, so if I might cut to the chase, remember two names for a quick-hit, long-blooming cure: 'Hampshire Purple', a compact groundcover up to one foot, and 'Brookside', with purple-blushed blue flowers, capable of growing to two to three feet.

But if you've done the genteel geranium thing and are looking for plants that pack more of a wallop, let's slow down and get cozy with several black-eyed beauties I think of as "The Three Faces of Ann."

'Ann Folkard' *(G. procurrens × G. psilostemon)*: 'Ann' begins the season clothed in deeply cut golden leaves—a nice start to the spring—and in full sun maintains a light-dappled glow to her foliage, which turns increasingly green with age. Her flowers are one-and-a-half-inch saucer-shaped beauties that begin as a dusky purple-magenta with a prominent black eye and then mellow to a more subdued hue. 'Ann' is gregarious and takes up a lot of room in the bed; though she's typically only one to two feet high, her long, thin stems are capable of stretching to five feet across. Variable in shape, she can make a superb mound (the more sun, the denser), or a frothy stream wending its

the facts

BOTANICAL NAME:
Geranium

SOUNDS LIKE:
Uranium

TYPE:
Summer-blooming perennial, often with good fall color

BASIC NEEDS:
Sun to part shade; average moisture and soil

WORST ENEMY:
Excess—whether sun and drought or dry shade

BEST ADVICE:
Don't throw a party without some

summer

way through the garden.

'Patricia' *(G. endressii × G. psilostemon)*:
Judging solely by their faces, you can certainly tell that 'Ann' and 'Patricia' are
sisters; they share the same dark *G.
psilostemon* eye. The major difference is
that 'Patricia' has more soft pink than
her showy magenta sibling, and she
uses an eyeliner more maroon than
black. In body type, however,
you'd never confuse them, since
'Patricia' very much favors her
dark-eyed parent, forming a
zaftig two-and-a-half-foot perennial
with extremely large green leaves. I recently saw both 'Patricia' and
her straight species parent and noticed a real, though subtle, difference: the offspring is slightly more pastel in complexion and has a
well-mannered form. I admit my own preference is for *G. psilostemon,* three feet by four feet and quite rude.

'Salome' *(G. procurrens × G. lambertii)*: She's the youngest of the
three; certainly, she's the fairest. Her face is smaller, softer, and more
refined, with five distinct petals to her flower, each washed in soft
violet and heavily veined in a deeper, darker shade. The veins flow
toward the center, staining the base of each petal for an overall
effect of dark eyes. Of the 'Ann' stepsisters — and there are others —
'Salome' is the most like her, with the same golden foliage in youth
and the same adventurous, rambling form. Ah, but while 'Ann' can
get wanton, 'Salome' keeps a low profile, content to hug rather than
conquer the ground. Because 'Salome' has the kind of sweet nature
that might make her the favorite, I wouldn't put them together: Ann
might ask for — and get! — Salome's head.

Geranium

8 5

Helianthemum

the facts

BOTANICAL NAME:
Helianthemum

SOUNDS LIKE:
Steely Dan undone

COMMON NAME:
Sunrose, rock rose

TYPE:
Ground-covering, summer-blooming perennial

BASIC NEEDS:
Full sun, extremely fast drainage

WORST ENEMY:
Shade

BEST ADVICE:
Ideal for a sunny hillside cover; don't let leaves from deciduous trees pile up on plants in fall

I'm not proud to admit that it's taken me years to sort out *Helianthemum* (sunrose), *Helenium* (sneezeweed), and *Helianthus* (sunflower). Not simply because all three names share the same sun-kissed prefix, but because the middle one reminds me of a plant I hate (the blanket flower, *Galliardia* 'Goblin', truly scary). This knee-jerk association, however unfair, has managed to prejudice me against all three of the "H" plants.

Nevertheless, I'm past all that. Now when I hear the word *Helianthemum,* I want whatever color I can get.

Here are some descriptive highlights from a plant catalog rife with sunrose selections: apricot yellow; double peach pink; warm tangerine; copper gold; deep crimson; salmon-shaded bronze; watermelon red. Other terms that crop up in descriptions of this genus as a whole are "drought-tolerant," "ground-covering," "weed-suppressing," and, most often, "easy." Yes, you do want this plant.

While the dozens, maybe hundreds, of helianthemum hybrids on the market vary in lusciousness, in flowering season they all sport bite-sized, saucer-shaped, crepe-paper-thin blossoms that smother the plants. Yellow stamens add a great deal of ornamentation, whether deepening a shade of apricot or igniting a dragon-breathing red.

Each color range is represented by a number of proven cultivars, but just as important is what you want in a leaf. We're talking ever-green foliage, after all, and not just straight green; a number of plants come clothed in soft gray. A colleague who shares my decided preference for the gray stuff has also found that the green-leaved forms don't hold up as well through winter, but neither of us should be credited with objectivity.

I can say that the gray-leaved sunrose I grow looks flawless all year long. I've no idea what cultivar it is, definitely nothing special, but after starting life in your basic four-inch pot, it's now a three-by-two-foot mat. Had I a dry border or a sunbaked parking strip, I would stuff it full of this reliably hardy genus. Which, incidentally, is despised by deer, who will then be driven to eat all your 'Goblins' — a just and proper thing.

H. 'Wisley Pink'

Helianthemum hybrids are often crosses among the species *H. apenninum*, *H. nummu-larium*, and *H. croceum*.

'St. Mary's':
White flowers; narrow, dark green leaves; likely to rebloom in September

'Wisley Pink' (syn. 'Rhodanthe Carneum'):
Pink icing on a resplendent cake; gray leaves

'Wisley Primrose':
The same cake with lemon frosting

'Cheviot':
Coral flowers; gray leaves (choice and hard to find)

'Mrs. Mold':
Deep bronzy salmon flowers; green leaves

'Henfield Brilliant':
Terra cotta to burnt orange flowers; gray leaves

'Orange Surprise':
Golden orange; green leaves

'Fire Ball':
Double scarlet pom-poms flecked gold; green leaves

Helianthemum

Itea ilicifolia

BROADLEAF EVERGREEN

the facts

BOTANICAL NAME:
Itea ilicifolia

SOUNDS LIKE:
Ikea illicit toll ya

COMMON NAME:
Hollyleaf sweetspire

TYPE:
Spreading, rounded ever-
green shrub; 6 to 8 feet

BASIC NEEDS:
Part sun, even moisture,
well-drained soil

WORST ENEMY:
Doesn't appreciate
Fahrenheit temperatures
in single digits

BEST ADVICE:
At its most handsome in a
warm, woodland nook

Itea ilicifolia in bloom appears naggingly familiar. One of our West Coast native garryas? Wouldn't rule it out, at least not from a distance. Holly? Has to be, look at those leaves. But all semblance of botanical certainty ends with a closer look at its flowers, foot-long catkins that drip off branch ends like Spanish moss.

In fact, the hollyleaf sweetspire is related to the flowering currant, *Ribes.* Unlike that late-winter-blooming deciduous shrub, the hollyleaf is a medium-sized evergreen that adds an unusual—and as it turns out, unfamiliar—complexity to the garden. Its presence is entirely memorable and continues to inspire me as I look at my own meager specimen and take solace in what the future will hold.

The plant's current struggle is my own fault. In the two and half years since it arrived in the mail, I've planted, uprooted, and replanted the thing three times. What I'm looking at now is a somewhat prostrate—though lustrous—spreading shrub wearing the first few flowers of its youth. I expect that once I make its final bed and let the poor thing lie in it, my *I. ilicifolia* will settle into its promised glory.

Sited in a cozy, partly shaded spot, out of harsh wind and where temperatures are kind (ideally, above 5°F), this lustrous plant can reach eight feet by eight feet. Mine was unaffected by a 15-degree cold spell at Christmas. Its leaves are spiny-toothed and dark green, surprisingly thin and pliable, and not nearly as lethal as those of some hollies. Though its glistening presence is fairly muted through the year—a rich, graceful backdrop in a mixed bed—the shrub begins to shimmer midsummer through fall, with sweetly fragrant, eight- to twelve-inch flowers that are like a tall drink of water on a hot August day.

Sunset magazine claims that the hollyleaf sweetspire is "not striking," but I beg to differ. It's simply a question of whether you want a plant to draw you into its mystery or blind you with its light. If your tastes run to the latter, and you need an evergreen with bright flowers, you might prefer *Escallonia*, another member of the family *Grossulariaceae*, which will give you show-stopping color. But if you're inclined to play with light and shadow and like atypical blossoms at unexpected times of year, this is the itea for you.

Except I forgot to mention one small thing: the deciduous Virginia sweetspire, *I. virginica*. To suggest that your first itea be *I. ilicifolia* would be like recommending Bach's solo cello suites to someone who has never heard his more exuberant orchestral works. The Virginia sweetspire's showy racemes of creamy white, fragrant spring flowers—combined with its brilliant reddish purple autumn leaves and eager, spreading habit—make it a must-have, basic repertoire garden item. So if you haven't tried *I. virginica*, ask for 'Henry's Garnet' at the nursery. And while you're at it, pick up the Brandenburg Concertos on your way home.

I. ilicifolia

Knautia macedonica

PERENNIAL

No doubt you've heard the old adage, "plants don't read." What a relief! I'd hate for the little red pincushion flower, *Knautia macedonica*, to unwittingly leaf through the perennials book I found on my shelf the other day, and discover its reputation trashed:

"A loosely erect, rather straggling plant . . . rarely grown . . . hardiness is somewhat uncertain." Don't you believe it! Knautia is hardy, popular, and perfectly willing to behave. You just need to know how to cajole it into keeping its mounded shape (instructions to follow). Otherwise ludicrously forgiving, it's the ultimate perennial for beginners, not to mention those of us who like to accessorize with color (outfits to follow, too).

To keep the plant respectable, give it a good haircut in late spring, then—as inelegantly as you dare—touch it up as the season progresses (that is, grab a handful of spent blossoms from time to time and chop). In full sun and very average soil, this deeply colored *Scabiosa* relative will be covered in white-anthered, crimson-purple flowers from early summer through late, late fall (my notes from 1996 list knautia as still in bloom on November 18).

K. macedonica's foliage is, frankly, unextraordinary, aside from the fact that two distinct leaf shapes—both entire and pinnately

K. macedonica

the facts

BOTANICAL NAME:
Knautia macedonica

SOUNDS LIKE:
Naughty a mass of Monica

COMMON NAME:
Red pincushion flower

TYPE:
Incredibly easy, impossibly long-blooming perennial

BASIC NEEDS:
Sun

WORST ENEMY:
Tendency to sprawl in too-rich soil or in shade

BEST ADVICE:
Cut back to 1 foot in late spring for a more compact plant

'Ruby Star':
Incredibly useful dwarf
form, 18 to 24 inches;
just introduced by Joy
Creek Nursery,
Scappoose, Oregon.

lobed—are found on any one plant. The secret of using this hard-working, two- to three-foot clumper artfully is to make the least of its foliage and the most of its burgundy baubles, as they weave on invisible stems mid-air.

Ensembles are unlimited. Punch it through silver foliage, lay it at the feet of chartreuse shrubs, let it play hide-and-seek through the powdery blue leaves of *Rosa glauca*. Or for the ambitious among you, consider this color combo featuring *K. macedonica*, from the perennial border at the Bellevue Botanical Garden east of Seattle (yes, you can try this at home): low, silvery swirls of *Artemisia canescens* made moody by the mahogany leaves of *Sedum* 'Moerchen', lit up by the chartreuse bells of *Nicotiana langsdorfii*, which speak to the lime leaves of *Geranium* 'Ann Folkard' (she of the black-eyed, magenta flowers), all topped off with the crimson-leaved Amazon queen, the castor bean *Ricinus* 'Carmencita'. Intense, huh?

But, admittedly, somewhat disparate, until you accessorize with *K. macedonica:* hundreds of bold, dark buttons poking through the silver, echoing the mahogany, shouting over to the chartreuse, comforting the black eye. Whoa! An extraordinary effect achieved by a workaholic little plant with a whole lot to prove.

Lagerstroemia

DECIDUOUS SHRUB OR TREE

the facts

BOTANICAL NAME:
Lagerstroemia

SOUNDS LIKE:
Bag a stream, Mia

COMMON NAME:
Crape myrtle

TYPE:
Multistemmed or single-trunked summer-flowering shrub or tree, 2 to 30 feet

BASIC NEEDS:
Every minute of available sun for best flowering; well-drained soil

WORST ENEMY:
Powdery mildew makes a mess of flowers; buy disease-resistant cultivars only

BEST ADVICE:
Beyond –5°F, you're heading for trouble; cutting back on water after July will increase hardiness and may promote bloom

Being guilty, as charged, of bringing an Easterner's perspective to Northwest horticulture, I freely admit that come late summer, I miss crape myrtles. From Philadelphia on south, they are then in peak bloom, their flowers like huge pink and purple rollers sprouting off the heads of trees.

Most of the truly superb varieties on the market are the work of the late horticulturist Donald Egolf, whose National Arboretum introductions are easily identified by their American Indian names. Working with two *Lagerstroemia* species, *L. indica* and *L. fauriei,* he bred for traits such as disease resistance, cold tolerance, colorful bark, and recurrent bloom. Hybridizing continues, but one crape myrtle trait remains constant: In order to flower, the plants need a long season of heat.

Presumably, that's why crape myrtles are in short supply in the Northwest. No one thinks they'll flower here because it's not hot enough, long enough. Which must be a real confidence killer for the local lagerstroemias who've been waiting for someone to notice them, fresh from the beauty parlor and decked out in full bloom.

Crape myrtles vary in size from the slow-growing, semidwarf 'Acoma', ultimately ten feet tall and multistemmed in habit, to the supercharged, two-story 'Natchez', with a mottled, peeling cinnamon bark as spectacular as its foot-long white flowers. All flower panicles are pyramidal in shape and come in both pastel and saturated colors, including 'Catawba', probably the darkest purple crape myrtle available, and 'Miami', with deep coral-pink blossoms. Breeding continues in pursuit of richer reds and regal purples.

Even if flowering is sporadic over the years—you might as well take it for granted, and avoid getting bent out of shape—the trunks on a number of cultivars are reason enough to give this plant a place in the garden. Crape myrtles can exfoliate (peel) with age, revealing an underbark that is mottled, splotched, spotted—you name it—in shades of cappuccino, silvery gray, and sycamore white. Adjectives like "muscular" and "sinewy" come to mind, much as for the genera *Stewartia* and *Parrotia*; the difference is you don't have to wait quite so long for these strip-tease trees to disrobe.

A few words about fall color: It all depends. The same tree might be bright orange-red one year and muddy brick the next, depending on the weather. For best color, trees like a long, slow, sunny, and gradually cold fall— circumstances blissfully beyond your control.

L. 'Zuni'

L. fauriei:
Forget flowers and grow this species for its bark. Ditto for the selections 'Fantasy', 'Kiowa', and 'Townhouse'.

'Zuni':
Medium lavender flowers, orange-red fall color, and a particularly successful bloomer in the Northwest, 9 feet

...and book now for the upcoming Crapemyrtlettes, pint-sized plants (e.g., the 2-foot 'Chickasaw') for container gardening.

Lagerstroemia

Pennisetum

Furry bottlebrush, fat foxtails, caterpillars on steroids—these are the flowers of *Pennisetum,* an ornamental grass that's apparently been crowded out by *Miscanthus,* given its conspicuous absence from our gardens. Enough! Time to yank that flopping gigunda grass and try something more in scale.

Let's start really small: *P. alopecuroides* 'Little Bunny'. This cultivar tops out at six inches and makes a diminutive grass mound topped by perky cottontail flowers. I've always hated this dollhouse reduction of the species, but nicer people think it's adorable. And I've never seen its variegated playmate 'Little Honey', but I reserve the right to scowl.

Knee-high, we've got *P. orientale.* Now this is some kind of plant: a foot-and-a-half mound of glaucous green foliage that sends up breathlessly pink pussytails in early July. *P. orientale* is blessed with the longest-lasting of all the fountain grass flowers; better yet, the pink takes a few months to fade. No need to fuss over it, just make sure it's got good drainage and adequate summer water. Be careful not to drown it when it's young.

At two feet, max, there's *P. villosum.* Think "vill" for "villain." Feathertop is considered a noxious weed in Southern California. But wait! Mike Smith at Joy Creek Nursery in Scappoose, Oregon, has been growing these white, feather-duster flowers for years and swears there's been no self-seeding (his friends don't believe him). Furthermore, Smith's feathertop (which he wears only to parties) has weathered 14°F, though it's not supposed to be hardy. The key, he says, is fast drainage.

Though the genus's tendency to self-seed is a very real problem in some places, it is not as big an issue in Oregon's Willamette Valley. The reason, say the grass-growing folks at American Ornamentals in Eagle Creek, is that the weather's all wrong for good germination by the time the seeds finally drop.

Now we've come to the giant of the genus, *P. alopecuroides* (one of my favorite Latin species names, rhyming with "I will peck your toy Ds"), a shower of bright green foliage with stiff foxtail flowers that tumble off the ends of the plant. It's capable of four feet, though typically shorter, and moves beautifully in a breeze, with creamy white to tan flowers in midsummer and leaves that turn golden in fall.

Two exceptional selections of this fountain grass have become staples of the trade: 'Hameln', at least a foot smaller, somewhat finer, and often earlier to flower; and 'Moudry', denser and coarser, with near-black plumes nestled in the foliage. The blooms don't even pretend to emerge till late September.

Finally, there's the pennisetum most likely to be prom queen, the purple-leaved *P. setaceum* 'Rubrum', phenomenally popular and grown an as annual coast to coast. This is one tender plant no one minds paying for (and pay you will), such is its value as an accent: a three- to four-foot lustrous mound of dark, sultry foliage with wine-red plumes. This is also the grass you're going to most regret losing should it not return next spring.

Carpe Pennisetum!

Phlomis

EVERGREEN SHRUB

If . . . you like lamb's ears but don't enjoy scraping squashed leaves off the pavement . . . you prefer the way perennials flower but you need an evergreen shrub . . . you've sworn never to water again . . . Grow *Phlomis*. It's as simple as that.

the facts

BOTANICAL NAME:
Phlomis

SOUNDS LIKE:
Flow this

COMMON NAME:
Jerusalem sage

TYPE:
Evergreen summer-
blooming perennial,
3 feet tall and as wide

BASIC NEEDS:
Full sun, fast drainage

WORST ENEMY:
Muck and shade

BEST ADVICE:
Even though you'll hate
to do it, cut back after
flowering to keep shapely

P. fruticosa

Species abound, with varying degrees of soft foliage, showy flowers, and shrubby habits, but if you're new to this genus, start with *P. fruticosa*, Jerusalem sage.

From the moment I put it into the ground — roughly two autumns ago — my *P. fruticosa* has not had a bad day. Whether skating through the thrills and chills of a 15°F cold snap or bathing in summer's full sun, this plant has simply grown and flowered and grown some more. Ironically, the worst it's ever looked is in bloom, bent with the weight of its own flowers. For that, I blame myself. I should have cut it back after flowering last summer, but it seemed so unnecessary then. Now I know.

This is what all the fuss is about: A three-foot, upright-to-sprawling clump of gray-green felted foliage, probably wider than tall, with furry, pale, square stems (read: mint family) that feel like pipe cleaners, and sheep-soft leaves. The leaf undersides, also pale, add a pronounced, two-tone stitching to the leaf margins. The plant has an overall soft, silvery presence, not at all coarse, just robust.

The flowers of *P. fruticosa* begin life fat and round (about the size of a ball you'd play jacks with) with two dozen closed flower buds crammed inside. These textured balls balance in the axils of the uppermost leaves, sometimes stacked one above the other. The buds are formed by April, begin flashing a little yellow in early May, and fully open to two-lipped, hooded flowers by June. Throw in a long bloom time, and we're talking a three-month bud-to-burst show.

What else? Ludicrously hardy, that's what. I'm not entirely sure what region of the Mediterranean it's native to, but this is clearly no fair-weather plant. Its origins also hint at its cultural preferences — hot sun, fast drainage — as well as implying its nature: No work and all play.

Most of these species are shrubby and evergreen:

P. aurea:
Golden downy leaves; to 3 feet

P. cashmeriana (Kashmir sage):
Large lilac-purple flowers and 3-foot downy leaves; 12° to 15°F

P. italica:
Finely textured, narrow leaves with pink flowers; resents winter wet; 1 foot; 12° to 15°F

P. lanata:
Small, fuzzy gray leaves tinged gold; deep yellow flowers; 2 feet; 12° to 15°F

P. purpurea:
Big woolly gray leaves and lilac-rose flowers; 2 feet; 12° to 15°F

P. russeliana:
Largest leaves, with bold, coarse habit and yellow summer flowers; 3 feet

And, if you're lucky enough to score this, buy me one too:

P. 'E. A. Bowles':
Robust hybrid of the yellow-flowering *P. fruticosa* and *P. russelliana*; supposed to be the best of both worlds

Phlomis

Phormium

EVERGREEN PERENNIAL

the facts

BOTANICAL NAME:
Phormium

SOUNDS LIKE:
Pour me rum

COMMON NAME:
New Zealand flax

TYPE:
Tender evergreen perennial,
1 to 8 feet

BASIC NEEDS:
Sun, summer water,
good drainage

WORST ENEMY:
Let's put it this way:
If the battery's dead from
cold, so's your plant; can
only cope with brief dips
under 15°F

BEST ADVICE:
In case of 20°F, swaddle
garden plants in burlap, or
dig up and bring in; not a
good bet for the hot and
humid Southeast

When the Maori left their native Polynesia centuries ago and settled in what is now New Zealand, they struck it rich with the native genus *Phormium.* It would now take an entire day of mall shopping to pick up all the stuff they made from this flax. We're talking fishing nets and baskets from its fibrous leaves, makeup from its pollen, and river rafts from its spent flower stalks.

We, on the other hand, have generally ignored the wonders of this evergreen perennial, worried that a bad winter might strike it dead (it can, and will). But today's stunning new hybrids are too good to pass up, even as pricey annuals, with their apricot, bright pink, or red bolts of lightning on dramatic, disease-resistant, mega-iris leaves.

Phormiums are unsurpassed as architectural plants. Their yucca-like structure and rainbow hues make them knockout single specimens, while several can add rhythm to an otherwise monotonous garden. Extremely evocative, they conjure a variety of landscapes, from arid to aquatic and on toward coconut heaven. In fact, phormium is so evocative that one good-sized specimen of the rich purple-leaved *P. tenax* 'Atropurpureum', with little more than a couple of shrub roses for company, can turn a ho-hum front yard into a tropical illusion.

In temperate West Coast climates these are big, I mean big, plants, so if eight feet scares you, aim lower. *P.* 'Tom Thumb', at two feet, has thick, undulating olive-green leaves with red-bronze edges, and looks like a sedge with thicker, twisted foliage. Smaller phormiums contrast beautifully with mounding perennials such as *Dianthus* and coral bells: picture the blushed-salmon tones of the more hardy hybrid 'Maori Maiden' arching over a plum-leaved *Heuchera.* Whooza.

Tension is an invaluable, if not exquisite, design element, and the larger flaxes create quite a stir while maintaining their stiff, fan-shaped composure. 'Sundowner' can grow five to six feet with particularly flat bronze-green fans and rosy margins that fade to pink and cream. The plant is a complete outrage associated with variegated shrubs. For high drama, bury the smaller, two-tone 'Apricot Queen' up to its knees in purple-foliaged sedum, and watch the neighborhood come alive.

Speaking of life—or in this case, sudden death—most hybrid phormiums are not as hardy as the straight species, *P. tenax* (which might survive a 15°F winter without dying back). An optimum scenario would be a site sheltered from the wind, with good drainage and a heavy mulch. Once temperatures fall to the mid-teens, I suggest you panic, run outside, pot up that puppy, and keep it in an unheated basement till all danger is past. Judging by how happy mine looked a month after rescue, your phormium will forgive and forget.

P. 'Sundowner'

Phygelius

Humans have done the natural world no favors when it comes to naming new varieties of plants. We've got enough 'Elf', 'Pixie', 'Baby', and 'Sweet Something' cultivars to saccharinize manure tea. The American nursery industry is convinced that unless a plant's name is 'Adorable', nobody's going to take it home. But who wants a plant purported to be innocuous, insubstantial, and dull?

So it's all the more delightful that an exhibitionist like *Phygelius* has managed to escape this nomenclatural humbug. The genus is blessed with appropriately evocative cultivar names that actually say something about the plant. 'Devil's Tears' has got to be red and pack a wallop; 'Salmon Leap'—what else but spirited and bright? 'African Queen'—exquisite and unapologetic. 'Tommy Knockers'—who knows, but it's definitely not cute.

Phygelius, or Cape fuchsia, is native to South Africa, a vast source of fabulous and temperate plants. Its name is thought to be from the Greek *phyge* as in "flight" or "avoidance," "in consequence of its having so long escaped the researches of botanists." That's according to the English botanist W. J. Hooker, who might have been kidding. (Then again, do botanists kid about this stuff?)

Perhaps not as funny, but even more preposterous, is how long-blooming this plant is: figure late spring sporadically through

the facts

BOTANICAL NAME:
Phygelius

SOUNDS LIKE:
Cornelius

COMMON NAME:
Cape fuchsia

TYPE:
Upright, airy subshrub or perennial; to 5 feet

BASIC NEEDS:
Sun to part shade; well-drained soil; drought tolerant

WORST ENEMY:
Shade

BEST ADVICE:
So much rhythm, color, and pleasure here, you must grow this plant

P. 'Winchester Fanfare'

November. Though there are subtle structural differences among cultivars, typically the individual flowers are two inches long, shaped like dangling tubular trumpets with slightly flared mouths (a veritable one-stop shop for hummers). They grow in eight- to ten-inch clusters at the top of upright flowering stems, which, once spent, can be cut back to six inches above the ground.

A compact, bushy, three- to five-foot semi-evergreen plant with shiny leaves, phygelius will multiply in width by sending out suckers. You can either yank them out or just let the beast go. The genus falls into that funny category, subshrubs—as do *Caryopteris* (bluebeard shrub) and hardy fuchsia—a clue to gardeners that during a particularly cold winter, the plant's stems may die back to the ground. Not to worry, it's hardy to 0°F and evergreen to 20°F, but a warm spot with good drainage couldn't hurt.

The only drawback I can think of to phygelius is having to choose a cultivar. Lack of availability narrows down the choice only a little, since most are easy enough to get your hands on and none could be described as rare. If I had to find a flaw, it would be with the lovely dwarf variety with dusty-coral tubes and a striped yellow throat. Better look away sheepishly when you ask for it by name: 'Pink Elf'.

gimme more

Phygelius × rectus cultivars:
'African Queen':
Crimson tubes, orange/red inside edges
'Devil's Tears':
Dark red in bud, glowing red tubes, orange/red edges
'Moonraker':
Pale yellow tubes, deeper yellow lobes
'Pink Elf':
Dusty coral tubes, red lobes, 2 feet
'Salmon Leap':
Pale salmon/orange tubes held at 45-degree angles
'Sensation':
Dusty magenta, unstoppable bloomer
'Sunshine':
The first Cape fuchsia with lime foliage
'Winchester Fanfare':
Dusky red/pink, very straight tubes, scarlet lobes

P. aequalis 'Yellow Trumpet':
Bushiest habit of the Cape fuchsias; pale yellow tubes

Phygelius

Salix elaeagnos

DECIDUOUS SHRUB

the facts

BOTANICAL NAME:
Salix elaeagnos

SOUNDS LIKE:
Hay licks Ellie Agnes

COMMON NAME:
Hoary or rosemary willow

TYPE:
Multistemmed shrub or
small tree, 8 feet

BASIC NEEDS:
Full sun, even moisture

WORST ENEMY:
Dry shade

BEST ADVICE:
A more refined
specimen when pruned
into tree form

Sometimes a plant just calls to you when you see it in the distance, like a stranger across a crowded room. And somehow you know, you know even then. . . . But because so many plants call to you, you promptly forget.

Until the second time you see the plant, and the same thing happens, though this time your pulse quickens as the recognition sets in. Yes! It's you! Wait, let me get a pen. Spell that for me, would you? You're kidding; you're a *willow?*

I can pretty much trace my romance with *Salix elaeagnos*, rosemary willow, to the perennial border at the Bellevue Botanical Garden near Seattle: A distinguished tall, lean, silver-gray plant, so textural I could feel the wind play its linear, tapered leaves. It looked hot-blooded, maybe from Chile or Mexico, but I've since found out it winters in the French Alps. After that first encounter, I made a mental note that this silver stream of light would one day sparkle in my garden.

Four years later we met again. Its leaves had lost none of their magic, and only then did I realize why it struck home. Its long, reaching fingers reminded me of the first foliage plant that ever turned my head. I know it only as "false aralia"—an indoor house plant that promised more intriguing leaves than that overgrown house pet, philodendron.

Since in the interim I had converted to foliage as a religion, this second sighting of the rosemary willow underscored my faith. In this incarnation, it was a six-foot-by-eight-foot openly pruned tree, rather than the goblet-shaped, multistemmed shrub you might expect a willow to be. I wouldn't call it a knockout structurally—the genus tends to be brittle—but combined in a shrub border with denser textures, it looks like tinsel on a tree.

On the East Coast, where the weather is more brutal, *S. elaeagnos* is typically cut to the ground on a regular basis to avoid legginess and promote long shoot growth. Treated like that, the shrub is a flickering mass of foliage, lightly textured but nonetheless quite dense. I prefer it pruned selectively like a small tree. This is more of a challenge for the gardener (read: work) and, admittedly, a gamble that may not pay off (dieback or cracked limbs could spoil your hard-pruned design).

You could also treat it the way they do at Bellevue, where it sits unpruned (except for branches that end up prone), like a silver lyre at the top of a hill. When you're at the bottom of the hill looking up, it doubles as an airy screen to hide the footpath within the border. The plant is set off to enormous advantage by the purple-black stems of the nearby shrubby dogwood, *Cornus kesselringii*, which distract you entirely come winter, when the willow has nothing to say.

After eight years, Bellevue's rosemary willow is seven feet by eight feet, which confirms what the fine print would tell you if you'd care to read it: This plant—as well as almost all the others sold under the same name—is in fact *S. elaeagnos* subsp. *angustifolia* and not the straight species (gasp!), which is a much larger growing and somewhat larger-leaved form.

S. elaeagnos

Salix elaeagnos

103

Sidalcea

the facts

BOTANICAL NAME:
Sidalcea

SOUNDS LIKE:
Did Al see ya

COMMON NAMES:
False mallow, prairie
mallow, checkerbloom

TYPE:
Summer-blooming
perennial

BASIC NEEDS:
Sun, well-drained soil, supplemental summer water

WORST ENEMY:
Rust; control with removal
of all infected leaves at first
signs of disease

BEST ADVICE:
Morning watering, room to
breathe, and good fall
cleanup prevent rust; make
way for clouds of butterflies

Sidalcea malviflora, the checkerbloom mallow, is an Oregon native that gardeners
in other regions knock themselves out
trying to grow. "Misery was its middle
name in the Armitage garden," writes
one of the country's leading perennial
experts, Allan Armitage, now living in
Georgia. Turns out all false mallows
hate heat and humidity (clearly,
they're discerning plants).

Here in the Northwest,
though, the genus thrives in
grasslands, in woodland
glades and by mountain
streams, where shrubby
plants averaging three
feet high flower in
pewtery pink through
deep rose. Think of
them as scaled-down,
long-blooming holly-
hocks, which is often
what the plants are
mistaken for, with their
small, rounded faces
cozied up cheek-to-
cheek on vertical racemes.

The species *S. oregana* is
readily found in the trade, a
three- to four-foot, deep-
rose, densely flowering native

S. malviflora 'Elsie Heugh'

which—depending on the subspecies—grows everywhere from sagebrush country to wet, grassy meadows and into the redwood forest. A naturally occurring variety is currently listed as an endangered species, *S. oregana* var. *calva,* as is Nelson's checkermallow, *S. nelsoniana.*

S. malviflora is a highly variable species ranging from Oregon to California. It has a stout, erect habit and funnel-shaped flowers up to two inches wide. You don't see the straight species for sale much, but its offspring are around; they are crosses of *S. malviflora* and the brilliant white prairie mallow *S. candida,* a two-foot native from Wyoming and Utah.

These crosses all produce similar hibiscus-like flowers, all in shades of pink. Unfortunately, as often happens when choosing variety names to describe this color, the nursery trade has a nasty habit of getting cloyingly sweet. Without further ado, here come the false mallow hybrids: 'Loveliness', 'Tenderness', and the truly unfortunate 'Party Girl', a good-looking, indefatigable plant with bright, sassy flowers. Probably the best-known sidalcea is the elegant three-foot *S.* 'Elsie Heugh', with heavily fringed petals on pale, satiny flowers. For height, the people's choice seems to be the four- to five-foot 'Sussex Beauty' and, for compactness, the two-foot 'Puck'.

All of the above fall somewhere between clear, soft, shell pink and rose pink, but for gardeners who like their color more assertive, there's also the carmine-red selection 'Brilliant'.

The sight of summer-blooming sidalceas, though hardly rare here, is far more common in European gardens. I read recently that the genus was "fast becoming better known . . . being profuse in flower, excellent for cutting, and of the easiest culture," but that was written in 1883. English plantsman William Robinson was always ahead of his time.

gimme more

S. campestris (meadow sidalcea):
1 foot pale pink flower; 5 feet

S. cusickii:
Rare; rose pink aging to deep purple; 5 feet

S. hendersonii:
Native to mud flats along the coast from British Columbia to California; 3.5 feet

S. hirtipes:
Larger flower, more saturated pink than *S. oregana*; flowers tighter on stem

S. malachroides (maple-leaved checkerbloom):
Woody perennial with grapelike leaves and white flowers

S. neomexicana:
Wide color range, from purple through white; 2 feet

Stachys

PERENNIAL

the facts

BOTANICAL NAME:
Stachys

SOUNDS LIKE:
Bacchus (or Take us)

COMMON NAME:
Lamb's ears

TYPE:
Summer-blooming perennial

BASIC NEEDS:
Sun and/or light afternoon shade, scant summer water, good drainage, lean soil

WORST ENEMY:
Slugs; bad drainage

BEST ADVICE:
S. albotomentosa (a.k.a. 'Hidalgo') if you need a nudge to try just one

Before there were Band-Aids, there was woundwort. This plant, with its large, soft leaves covered in fuzzy, soft-as-lamb's-ears hairs, was used to encourage blood clotting when wrapped around a cut. Native to the rocky hillsides of northern Turkey, woundwort could be found growing in lean-soiled, time-forgotten spots.

Today it spills over urban curbsides, crevices, and walkways and is often fondled but never worn. It is tenacious and aggressive but so incredibly adorable you can't resist putting one in the garden. In fact, lamb's ears has a lot in common with my little beagle, Della, who starts the evening softly curled in the corner, then stealthily creeps across the landscape and by morning has commandeered the bed.

Lamb's ears, how we love you! So soft, so silver, so sweet. Why must you rot out in wet winters and waste your stalks with boring blooms? No matter. Growing *Stachys byzantina* is a gardener's rite of passage, and for a challenging spot—such as a parking strip—this plant is a doer.

But the genus *Stachys* is not simply about furry leaves and washed-out-mauve flowers. We're talking showy, long-blooming ornamentals in pinks, purples, peaches, and corals. Turns out there are between two and three hundred species in this mint-family member, among the best known, big betony or *S. macrantha* (syn. *S. grandiflora*), an atypically green-leaved, pink-flowered, two-foot plant that makes an impressive foliage mass. This big-flowered form comes in an even showier color, too—the deep violet 'Superba'—with dense whorls of blossoms rising eight inches above heart-shaped, toothed foliage.

Two species boast small, soft fruit-punch flowers. The first is the rich-scarlet-to-coral-dipped *S. coccinea*, reminiscent of some Mexican salvias (it happens to be native to Mexico and parts of the South-west) and a complete heart-stopper in summer. It has neat, one-inch triangular leaves, a slightly weaving habit, and wonderful flowers in loose whorls at the ends of its square stems.

My own favorite from Mexico is *S. albotomentosa* (often referred to by the cultivar name 'Hidalgo' after its place of origin), so closely related to *S. coccinea* that some consider it a subspecies. Fortunately, that's not your worry; you just need to find this great plant. 'Hidalgo' is a lamb lover's dream, with white-backed, felted gray-green foliage, tomentose (furry) stems and — wait for them — translucent coral flowers on tall stems. Oh, my.

The plant makes a dense mass, twice as wide as high, and flowers from June into November. But before you order a dozen, you should know that it's a slightly tender perennial, proven hardy to 15°F (though my guess is that with great drainage you could push it more).

Lastly, one for you rock gardeners: *S. corsica minus* is a delightful matting miniature, with dark green scalloped edges and waffle-textured leaves. Midsummer, when little else is in bloom, up pop three-inch deep pink flower spikes. Don't be fooled by a so-called dwarf *S. densiflora* that fits this same description. There ain't no such thing! It's *S. corsica minus*, which loves full sun, sharp drainage, and a crevice to call its own.

S. albotomentosa

For the petting zoo, *S. byzantina* cultivars, from 12 to 18 inches tall:

'Cotton Boll':
Lambsy leaves with flower spikes covered with fat, purple-gray buds

'Big Ears' (formerly 'Countess Von Zeppelin'):
Carpeting plant with enormous, felted gray-green leaves; less susceptible to summer meltdown and water-logged rot.

'Primrose Heron' and 'Limelight':
Velvet leaves emerge chartreuse, fade to light yellow-green; dead-head flowers to promote vigor.

Stachys

S. pseudocamellia

Stewartia

DECIDUOUS TREE

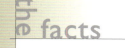

the facts

BOTANICAL NAME:
Stewartia

SOUNDS LIKE:
La Guardia

TYPE:
Elegant, mid-size, summer-flowering deciduous tree, 15 to 40 feet

BASIC NEEDS:
Think woodland: rich, evenly moist soil and protection from afternoon sun

WORST ENEMY:
Dry shade

BEST ADVICE:
It hates being moved, so choose the right spot carefully; I'd give this tree a starring role in any setting, large or small

Gilbert and Sullivan were all tra-la about the flowers that bloom in the spring, but I don't recall *The Mikado* paying much homage to the trees that bloomed in early summer. That seems quite an oversight for an operetta set in Japan, where beech forests pop white with the blossoms of *Stewartia,* an Empress among June-flowering trees.

Not only is *S. monadelpha,* or tall stewartia, an impressive eighty feet in the wild, this richly draped, orange-barked beauty has a trick up her sleeve. Edward Menninger, in his 1967 charmer of a book, *Fantastic Trees,* describes her as one of the "strip-tease trees." You ain't seen nothing till you've seen *S. monadelpha* shed those robes.

It's a promiscuous trait shared by nearly all stewartia species. With age, they lose their outer bark to reveal an inner glow of satin-smooth, camouflage-colored patterns, along with some incredibly sinewy, hard-body trunks that ripple under your touch (somebody stop me).

S. monadelpha seems to top out at thirty feet in urban gardens, where it comes into its own in a lightly shaded woodland planting. Just don't waste its peeling bark in a spot you only see as you mow by. The one-inch flowers on this species are the least conspicuous of the genus, but its fall color—ranging in shades from smoky yellow to orange and bright red—its tiered branching habit, and its rich, peeling, orange to cinnamon bark make it an outstanding specimen.

Drenched to the skin in our Northwest rain, orangebark stewartia is actually a great deal more beautiful here than it is on the East Coast, where the most popular stewartia is the twenty to thirty foot *S. pseudocamellia,* the Japanese stewartia. Its species name pretty much sums up the plant's great appeal: Each three-inch, cup-shaped, bright white flower with its contrasting orange anthers, bears a close resemblance to a single white camellia in bloom. On a hot, green, breezeless day in mid-June (isn't that an oxymoron in the Northwest?), the blossoms are like ice on the wrist.

The Japanese stewartia takes more sun than the orangebark, but still needs protection from the hot afternoon rays and likes its roots shaded and cool. Its bark is celebrated as the most colorful in the genus, in peeled-off patches of olive, tan, orange and white, and just as stimulating to the touch. This one's for the long haul gardener, though, since it may be a few decades before the trunk dramatically peels. Its fall color range is touted as everything from flaming crimson-yellow to glossy oranges, reds and purples, proving that parentage and environment make fall color pretty much a crap shoot.

S. pseudocamellia var. *koreana* (or *S. koreana,* still a taxonomic blur) is a more upright version of the Japanese stewartia. It's distinguished by heavily textured foliage and zigzagging branches that enhance its winter silhouette, plus irregularly flaking bark that reveals mottled shades of olive, cinnamon and gray. The flowers on the Korean stewartia are larger and more saucer-shaped than those of the pseudo-camelia.

For the best flowers, though, you'll have to trade off bark and worry a bit more about culture. *S. ovata,* known as mountain camellia or summer dogwood in its North Carolina-to-Florida homeland, has the largest flowers in the genus but needs a particularly wooded, evenly moist spot to thrive. It's late blooming and makes a spectacle of itself in fall, but gives away nothing come winter. The naturally occurring variety, *S. ovata* var. *grandiflora,* similarly strip-tease shy, is even more superbly flowered, with contrasting purple stamens. If your woodland garden is bereft of summer music, either of these G-rated July bloomers will happily make itself heard.

gimme more

S. malacodendron:
Flowers have purple stamens and steely blue anthers; this tree likes heat; 20 feet.

And the winner in the trendiest, rarest-in-cultivation category is:

S. rostrata:
With late-June flowers set off by deep ruby red bracts and 1-inch red seedpods that linger from summer through fall.

Stewartia

Stipa gigantea

Do me a favor. In June, go outside and take a good look at your garden.

Got enough flowers? Thought so. After all, it's June.

Got enough contrast between your plant shapes, like spiky vs. mounding stuff, fountain shapes, and climbers? Well done.

Now: Is anything moving? That's right, moving, as in wafting, weaving or waving in the breeze? Doesn't matter if it's not windy, just the slightest breath will do.

No? Okay, last question. Got any room left near the front of the bed? Come on, just four square feet? Atta girl, get out that spade. Do I have a plant for you.

Stipa gigantea has got to be one of the most kinetic marvels of the garden. It was easily the most touched and talked-about plant in my last yard, stopping kids, dog-walkers, and all manner of dawdlers, as it waved its welcome from either side of the front steps. Its tall, see-through wands rose out of nowhere, and—much like our corner neighbors who waved to every passerby—it always nodded hello.

Of course there might have been a whole lot more arm-waving had I not stupidly yanked out the developing flowering stalks in March (beware the impatient gardener). But the plants forgave me and kept up a happy appearance well into fall.

The giant feather grass is native to Spain and the mountains of Portugal, where it must make quite a sight at sunset, its flower spikes dripping in long, silken oats that ignite with an intense golden glow. These loose, open-flowering panicles hang from sturdy, arching stems called culms, which stand five to seven feet above your basic knee-high ornamental grass mound. The plant's compact shape, save for the culms, makes it easy to fit into the garden, and because its tall flower spikes are entirely see-through, even in the front of the border they never get in the way.

Instead, they almost frame the scenery around and behind them,

the facts

BOTANICAL NAME:
Stipa gigantea

SOUNDS LIKE:
Wipe a (or steep a)
pie pan t'ya

COMMON NAME:
Giant feather grass

TYPE:
June-blooming ornamental
grass

BASIC NEEDS:
Well-drained soil, full sun

WORST ENEMY:
Heavy rains may lay it flat
for some time

BEST ADVICE:
Site it along the walkway if
you want to make friends

moving the eye back and forth across the landscape as the hypnotic stems sway. Taking up little space, yet adding a great deal of depth and dimension, *S. gigantea* works either as a centerpiece in a tiny garden or as an accent in a vast border. Just be sure to site it where you can caress its fine head.

Ideally, you'll want to view your feather grass backlit, in order to make the most of its transparent, light-catching color. Along with other movers and shakers such as *Molinia* 'Windspiel' and 'Skyracer' (tall purple moor grass) and the summer-blooming *Dierama pulcherrimum* (wandflower), it's a plant that can take a little breeze and turn it into mobile art.

S. gigantea

S. arundinacea (pheasant grass): Upright, shiny grass blades that develop rich orange and red colors; open, airy panicles; sun to part shade. 2 feet by 3 feet. Said to self-seed (and what a pleasure that would be); marginally hardy, so treat as an annual to avoid severe disappointment.

S. capillata (feather grass): Finely textured clumping grass; gorgeous arching panicles that look like spun glass; 3 feet by 2 feet; great for arrangements.

S. tenuissima (syn. Nassella tenuissima) (Mexican feather grass): Silky, showy flowers like a blonde mane rising above wispy, fine foliage; 1.5 feet by 1.5 feet. Amazing massed, which it'll do itself (short-lived but vigorously self-seeding). Be careful of invasion where summers are wet.

Stipa gigantea

Thalictrum

PERENNIAL

History does not celebrate *Thalictrum*. You will find no Wars of the Rues. This plant has a gentle presence, unlikely to agitate or offend. In fact, if meadow rue were a woman, she'd be strikingly ethereal and often alone, lost in a great romance classic, probably *Gone With the Wind*.

As I think about it, I remember knowing a thalictrum in fourth grade. Her name was Victoria, and we were both ten. She was soft-spoken, with a nearly transparent complexion, and her heart belonged to Tara. But she lived behind a bowling alley in a tough part of town and that's probably why I liked her, knowing that for all her apparent daintiness she was a creature of far more durable stuff.

If Victoria were a thalictrum, she'd be *T. rochebruni-anum*, a species of great delicacy, with wiry purple stems topped by airy panicles of flowers like light lavender beads. Though appearing insubstantial, the plant's four- to six-foot stems are thicker than those of most thalictrums, and its June flowers are among the earliest. Its lack of density—which is not to say lack of intrigue—makes it a great foreground plant, inviting a closer look.

Then again, Victoria might also pass for the lavender *T. delavayi*, or better yet its white cultivar 'Album', a meadow rue with baby's breath–like flowers creating an ephemeral, see-through haze. While the foliage of *T. rochebrunianum* is blue-green and columbine-like, *T. delavayi* has decidedly bright green leaves that more closely resemble those of a maidenhair fern. Despite its delicacy, *T. delavayi* is the larger plant, growing to an astonishing seven feet. The variety least like Victoria would be 'Hewitt's Double', a once-rare, double-flowering form, now all the rage, with long-lasting lavender flowers.

Incidentally, should you come across a meadow rue named *T. dipterocarpum* while you're out shopping, go for it. This and *T. delavayi* are so similar, you'd need a ten-power magnifier to appreciate the difference. I've aggravated myself enough over this distinction, so you needn't bother.

The least known of the meadow rues are the dwarf species, including the irrefutably charming *T. kiusianum* and the steely blue *T. isopyroides*. *T. kiusianum* is a Japanese miniature species with the maidenhair-like foliage of other thalictrums, but on a teeny plant only four to six inches high. Once established, it will become a carpet of foamy, soft purple flowers blooming all summer long, but slugs adore its juvenile foliage, so you'll need to bait this baby. You should also know that it grows very slowly; best to divide its one-inch tubers when the plant's dormant, to help it crawl along.

T. isopyroides (sounds like I sew/buy doilies) is a superb one-foot foliage plant. We'll just skip the flowers. Each plant makes a dense mound of strikingly blue lacy leaves and is quite the foil for big-leaved, shade-loving plants, particulary hostas. Combining the two brings to mind a friendship between two ten-year-olds, one graceful and unsullied, the other a messy, freckle-faced chubpot. Guess which one was me.

gimme more

T. aquilegifolium (columbine meadow rue): Foamy pink flowers; 4 feet

T. flavum var. glaucum (dusty meadow rue): Blue foliage, yellow flowers; better for sun, 5 feet

T. dasycarpum (native meadow rue): Lavender tinged white flowers; 5 feet

T. rochebrunianum

Thalictrum

113

Trachycarpus

HARDY PALM

the facts

BOTANICAL NAME:
Trachycarpus

SOUNDS LIKE:
Take this carcass

COMMON NAME:
Windmill palm

TYPE:
Bristly trunked, jagged-
leaved, hardy palm

BASIC NEEDS:
Sun to part shade,
well-drained soil

WORST ENEMY:
Leaf-shredding winds,
bad drainage

BEST ADVICE:
Buy as large as you can
afford, plant in spring, and
remember: location,
location, location

Tropical, tropical, tropical. I know, I'm a broken record. But does anyone really enjoy schlepping tree ferns and striped bananas in and out of the house? Let's stop the madness right now and consider this question: Why grow the flora of South Africa, Indonesia, or Brazil?

Because we can! (Walked right into that, didn't you?) So-called tropicals can do wondrous things to a dusky, damp garden, and I say so-called because some of the showiest plants are hardy.

For my money, palms are the way to go. Biggest bang for the buck: *Trachycarpus fortunei*, the windmill palm. It thrives in cool, moist weather, will stick it out to 0°F, and, although slow-growing, is capable of fifteen to twenty feet. The tree has no special soil requirements or major pest problems and puts out its huge, corrugated palmate leaves in both sun and part shade.

The only thing you have to do is site the windmill palm carefully, because the leaves look quite the mess once shredded by cold winds. Check out your microclimates and try to protect it from northern and western blows. But don't sweat it if a few fans get ratty, because new ones will soon take their place; the old ones will simply fall and put another distinguishing notch in the tree's trademark bristly brown trunk.

T. fortunei ranks among the hardiest of the arborescent, or trunking, palms. But there's another ersatz tropical that takes even more

Trachycarpus takil:
This is the one for you if you like your hardy palms to play hard-to-get. Arguably a form of *T. fortunei*, this rarer selection is a taller, more robust form (albeit slower growing).

cold. *Rhapidophyllum hystrix*, the needle palm, is an East Coast native found as far west as Mississippi. It's more of a three- to four-foot clumper, with short, fat, pincushioned stems stuck with six- to eight-inch black spines. It's got your basic, deeply divided elephant-fan foliage, but its leaves are distinguished by their shimmering, silvery undersides.

No need to throw blankets over this baby in winter, though you might consider hauling them out in summer. *R. hystrix* likes it hot. It's happy to grow once the temperatures hit 85°F, but in Portland, Oregon, we've got only a few months of that. The trick here is to site it someplace well-drained, warm, and cozy (such as a southwest-facing corner that traps heat), then fertilize in early summer and keep it evenly moist.

Same goes for the dwarf palmetto, *Sabal minor*, another East Coast native with an inexplicable fondness for Oklahoma, where it has become the stuff of a small cottage industry: palmetto leaf brooms. *S. minor*'s huge palm fronds appear to rise directly out of the ground; they're blue-green, partially ribbed, and sometimes a whopping four inches across. The genus is represented by more than a dozen different species, but *S. minor* is probably the best choice for cool-to-cold-climate gardeners. Good to below zero but, again, hardiness is not the issue. It needs heat.

Of course, for palm-deprived readers in Bend, Oregon, hardiness is very much the issue. I don't want to raise false hopes, but I've recently read about a selection of scrub palm called *S. minor* 'McCurtain' offered by Plant Delights Nursery in Raleigh, North Carolina. It's alleged to have survived temperatures of –24°F in Wichita, Kansas, so it bears keeping an eye on. Otherwise, either console yourself with some of the gorgeous new variegated yuccas, or, my friend, prepare to schlep.

Trachycarpus

Verbascum

BIENNIAL OR PERENNIAL

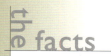
Her name is worth millions. With that and a few pence, the girl can buy a cuppa.

At least a decade ago, Helen Johnson, then a staff propagator at Kew Gardens in southwest London, had in her care a chance *Verbascum* seedling. It was a rather soft peach but with strong copper highlights and a central purple stain. It had matching purple filaments and brick-orange anthers that echoed the flower's complex sheen. This mullein was, in a word, stunning.

After being convinced of its worth, Kew Gardens worked out a royalties deal with the English nursery Hopley's to introduce this color breakthrough of a hybrid to the trade. The verbascum was named *V.* 'Helen Johnson' and is now sold worldwide, making good money for who-knows-how-many tens of thousands of growers (I have no idea whether it's still making money for Kew).

Helen, however, doesn't get a dime. After all, she was a paid employee. What she does get is a place in the hearts of all who've witnessed this plant in flower.

You go, Helen!

What an astonishingly sumptuous verbascum. Pure indulgence. And with a color that keeps coming, even after it slips away into soft mauve. I hear it's a short-lived perennial, and if I didn't know better I'd say that was planned obsolescence. You better believe I'll replace this plant.

But the only plan behind the brief life of 'Helen Johnson' is the Divine kind; short lives are the hallmark of the genus *Verbascum*. Some species are annual, others perennial, but primarily they tend to be biennial (read: blooming in their second year and then dying). In the case of the hybrids (which, in addition to our Helen, include such beauties as the double-clotted 'Cotswold Cream' and the purple-bellied 'Cotswold Queen'), three years may qualify as a full life.

Fortunately, these sterile hybrids can be rooted from cuttings, and the biennial species will self-seed if they're happy. Quite a few verbascums are worth growing for their foliage alone, including *V. bombyciferum* (Turkish mullein, not a reliable common name since several other verbascums are also from Turkey), with rosettes so densely white and woolly that they make lamb's ears look sheared. The leaves are anywhere from twelve to eighteen inches long, with almost no trace of gray in youth. By year two, the effect is somewhat less pristine but just as arresting, when the plant sends up a four- to six-foot cotton-covered spike. The yellow flowers that open later are a pleasant end to the show.

The other well-known folial wonder is *V. olympicum,* with white, woolly basal rosettes reaching three feet across. In flower, it's the very definition of a candelabrum, with white branching stems holding two- to three-foot panicles of bright yellow flowers. If deadheaded, there's a chance it'll flower again in fall.

A third, lesser-known species is *V. wiedemannianum,* which flowers in shades of salmon through violet and—I can confirm this—indigo blue. It's a great choice if you think of the yellow-flowered mulleins as roadside weeds. (Incidentally, the genuine weed is *V. thapsus,* an incredibly utilitarian plant but ratty all the same.) The violet-flowered species has huge tapered leaves covered by a cobweb of gray-white hairs, with flowering stalks anywhere from two to four feet high.

Lastly, a verbascum rivaled only by our Helen, *V. chaixii* 'Album': foot-high candles dripping with luxurious white flowers made striking by warm violet eyes. Unlike her copper-toned cousin, 'Album' makes the most of her wild oats; leave her be, and watch her sow.

Here are a couple of woody ones, each needs fast drainage:

V. dumulosum and V. 'Letitia':
Both are dense, rounded, and under a foot high. They have gray felted leaves and clear yellow flowers, and make great rock garden plants.

V. 'Golden Wings':
Similar in shape and habit but slightly larger (to 18 inches), with orange buds opening to yellow flowers.

V. 'Helen Johnson'

Verbascum

Vitex agnus-castus

DECIDUOUS SHRUB

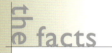
BOTANICAL NAME:
Vitex agnus-castus

SOUNDS LIKE:
Buy decks and use fastest

COMMON NAME:
Chaste tree

TYPE:
Large shrub or small deciduous tree with open, airy-
spreading habit, 10 feet

BASIC NEEDS:
Full sun, good drainage;
drought-tolerant
once established

WORST ENEMIES:
Impatience: plant leafs out
late, so don't yank it by
mistake; shade

BEST ADVICE:
To increase hardiness,
give it well-drained soil,
shelter it from wind, and
don't water after July;
expect limbs to be cut back
by prolonged cold

V. agnus-castus

The first thing you need to know about the chaste tree, *Vitex agnus-castus,* is that its foliage bears a striking resemblance to that of *Cannabis.* Growing it might be a cheap thrill for some or a source of worry for others, depending on how strongly you covet that elusive last laugh.

The second thing you might like to know is that the shrub's been highly touted for its effectiveness in regulating menstrual cycles and relieving symptoms of PMS (I recently stumbled across a book titled *Vitex: The Women's Herb*). It also has a positively ancient reputation as a sexual suppressant, one that Athenian women used to keep themselves chaste while in frenzied worship of the Greek goddess of harvests. According to the Roman naturalist Pliny, the celebrants "made their pallets and beds with the leaves thereof to cool the heat of lust."

And it wasn't just the ladies. Southern European monks are said to have brewed libido-busting tea from the shrub's fruit—hence its other common name, monk's pepper (talk about your condiments).

But it's the most innocent of pleasures that has led me to the chaste tree—its performance in the late-summer garden. This woody verbena relative can play a role easily as dynamic as those of *Buddleia davidii* (butterfly bush), *Hibiscus syriacus* (rose of Sharon), *Campsis radicans* (trumpet vine), and *Caryopteris* × *clandonensis* (bluemist shrub).

Anything but chaste in appearance, vitex has all the angles, with a multiple-stemmed symmetry enhanced by tapered, five-fingered leaves and jaunty eight-inch flower spikes of the softest lilac blue. It's a shrub that seems always in motion, what with the aerial high jinx of dive-bombing hummingbirds and silver-backed foliage that flickers in the wind. Though vitex is capable of at least ten feet if left unpruned (or better yet, limbed up like a tree), it can also be treated as a perennial and cut back to the ground each spring (like *Buddleia*, it flowers on new wood).

Chaste tree is a Mediterranean native and, as such, prefers life sunny and well-drained. Though it's drought tolerant once established, it will grow faster with supplemental summer water. Still, given the modesty of these cultural requirements, it's surprising the plant isn't more of a staple in the low-maintenance garden (and that its cultivars are so difficult to find). My best guess is that the chaste tree is a hard sell in spring, when it's more stick than shrub with no sign of green. Even an experienced gardener might mistake it for dead up until June, since it's predictably late to leaf out. Alas, by the time it's really cruising, most gardeners are finished buying shrubs.

But why? Late summer's a particularly good time to reassess the garden and fortify areas of complete boredom or excessive visual heat with bolts of cooling blue—not to mention a hit of sentimentality. Consider vitex a flashback to more acrid-odored times, when "hooch" meant more than Turner's partner, and libidos, like fertile goddesses, ran wild.

gimme more

Sure, just don't smoke it.

V. agnus-castus cultivars:
'Shoal's Creek':
Similar to species
'Silver Spire':
White form with pewter overtones
'Rosea':
Pink flowers

V. agnus-castus var. latifolia:
More robust grower, broader leaflets

V. negundo:
Larger, hardier species; flowers less showy but airier; to −10°F
'Heterophylla' (syn. V. incisa):
Hardiest of the vitex, with particularly refined, lacy foliage; to −20°F

Vitex agnus-castus

Zauschneria californica

EVERGREEN PERENNIAL

Sometimes I feel more like a *schadchen*—that's Yiddish for a professional matchmaker—than a garden writer. After all, we are both but humble intermediaries, each paid to introduce our clients to unimagined pleasures that were in plain sight all along. I say this because it's entirely likely you've already laid eyes on the California fuchsia. Perhaps you'd just never dreamed such flamboyance might be yours.

The genus *Zauschneria*—now reclassified as *Epilobium*, but don't get me started—is a member of the evening primrose family, though its flowers are far from mellow yellow. Instead, these inch-and-a-half-long firecrackers range in intensity from burning embers to a four-alarm blaze. The spectrum begins at the soft end with peachy pink and moves through salmon-orange on to lipstick red—colors that might blind us during softer times of the year but vibrate brilliantly in summer and fall.

Zauschneria's ratio of flower to foliage is part of the secret of its blazing success; its blossoms hover like punch-drunk hummingbirds above a spreading nest of green. In fact, hummers are guaranteed should a plant peek out from a rock wall or cavort on a sunny bank; they might even chance a drink along the sidewalk if this nectar-rich genus is left to scramble along a parking-strip edge.

Less certain is what your California fuchsia will look like if you buy the straight species, *Z. californica*. Variation is the rule, with leaves ranging from bright green to silvery gray and flowers from pink to scarlet. Named cultivars and selections are the way to go (though be warned, even these names can get confused). Among those getting consistently rave reviews are *Zauschneria* 'U. C. Hybrid' (syn. 'Rogers Hybrid'), with particularly impressive silver-gray foliage that holds up all season; *Z.* 'Mattole Select', a strong, silvery spreader with salmon-kissed scarlet

the facts

BOTANICAL NAME:
Zauschneria californica

SOUNDS LIKE:
Dowse sherry 'ya

COMMON NAME:
California fuchsia

TYPE:
Summer-blooming perennial or subshrub, 1 to 2 feet

BASIC NEEDS:
Full sun; excellent drainage; drought-tolerant

WORST ENEMY:
Bloom can be affected by early frost and heavy rains

BEST ADVICE:
Hot, dry, neglect, neglect, neglect; hardier in dry climates (to −10°F, easily) than in sodden ones

flowers held tightly against the foliage; and Z. 'Everett's Choice', a low-growing, profuse bloomer and the best choice for mass planting.

Despite its common name, California fuchsia is perfectly hardy in places as cold as Denver. Most zauschnerias here in Western Oregon will flourish, but the best bet for gardeners in harsher climates is the bright red species *Z. arizonica* (syn. *Z. californica* subsp. *latifolia* 'Arizonica'). This is a robust, shrubby form capable of two to three feet, and a favorite of that undaunted Rocky Mountain gardener and garden-book author Lauren Springer.

More important than temperature, however, is culture. This plant needs superb drainage, lean (vs. clay) soil, and the hands-down hottest spot in the garden. Meet these demands and zauschneria will dazzle you with years of passionate pleasure. Arranged marriages just don't get much better than that.

Z. californica

gimme more

Z. *californica* culitvars:
'Alba':
Fresh green foliage, white flowers; 8 inches by 2 feet

'Solidarity Pink':
Unusual color; may be more difficult to grow well; 1 foot by 2 feet

'Wayne's Silver':
One of many U. C. Berkeley forms with silver foliage, scarlet flowers; 1 foot by 3 feet

Z. 'Bowman':
Stiff, upright form particularly resilient in wet weather; 1.5 to 2 feet by 2 feet

Z. *californica* subsp. *latifolia*:
Narrow, felty leaves and scarlet trumpets on lax stems; probably the most robust variety in the Maritime Northwest.

Z. *septentrionalis*:
Tight, low mat of two-tone gray-green foliage; 8 inches by 18 inches.

fall

Acidanthera

BULBOUS PLANT

the facts

I could hardly wait to tell you about *Acidanthera bicolor* var. *murielae* (syn. *Gladiolus callianthus* 'Muriaelae'). Believe you me, the pleasure is all mine. From the highlands of Ethiopia to the sandy loam of Canby, Oregon, the planet is all the sweeter for its smell. Doesn't matter how hot the day, crabby the mood, or disheveled the garden; its soft and sugary fragrance obliterates place and time.

I discovered the peacock orchid (don't let the common name mislead you, this is a gladiolus) at Fragrant Garden Nursery in Canby in September, the same day my friend Esther and I overdid it big time at a dahlia ranch down the road. What a relief it was to soothe our retinas with this delicately tissue-petaled flower.

Save for its deliciously purple throat, the blossom itself is unaffected and unmistakable, like a white, spread-winged origami poised midflight. It dives from an arching stem, each stem producing six to ten flowers, which bloom in succession like a long-playing daylily, one flower lasting several days. Visualize that multiplied by dozens of stems—this flower begs for massing—and you've got about a month of gently perfumed skydiving swans.

The foliage is fresh green, ribbed, and sword-shaped, two to three feet high, emerging fairly late in the season (mine were planted in early spring, and didn't show growth till June). In less than full sun and less than fast drainage, the irislike leaves may bend, but the flower stems will be no less showy, even if the effect is not quite so pristine.

The ensemble is grace itself, particularly for a gladiolus; no "froufrouescence," as my friend Sean would say. And the big bonus is the late bloom time, from mid-August to mid-September—early enough to catch lingering summer-blooming perennials, late enough to usher in the newcomers of fall.

Clearly, you need this plant. The trick is growing it. In regions where winter temperatures are major league, plant acidantheras in

April, then lift in fall and overwinter in paper bags. In more temperate regions, they should be hardy barring a catastrophic winter (read: 10°F). In the maritime Northwest, a greater challenge is preventing rot; the best advice I've heard is to top your already well-drained soil with several inches of sand or gravel and plant directly in that.

How much can you lose? Maybe $7.50 for a handful or two of bulbs. Pretty good odds for pure joy.

A. bicolor

Aronia

DECIDUOUS SHRUB

the facts

BOTANICAL NAME:
Aronia

SOUNDS LIKE:
Baloney uh

COMMON NAME:
Chokeberry

TYPE:
Upright and arching, thicket-forming deciduous shrub; 4 to 8 feet

BASIC NEEDS:
Sun to light shade; adaptable to wet and dry soils

WORST ENEMY:
Shade causes excessive legginess and results in poor fruiting

BEST ADVICE:
Use a specimen to give height to a border without sacrificing depth, or mass in an informal setting

Fall is tough on the vocabulary of a garden writer. I don't think I have another riotous, spectacular, or gorgeous left to describe all these autumn leaves. But with one last gasp of superlatives, let me introduce the chokeberry, its common name a reference to its tendency to make birds gag. Honest.

Aronia is not in our winged friends' preferred food group. They tend to disdain its tough, astringent fruits until they've picked everything else clean. Which is precisely what makes chokeberry a good fall and winter ornamental: gobs of berries continue to glow well after its leaves have fallen.

You have three color choices in aronia berries: red *(A. arbutifolia)*, black *(A. melanocarpa)*, and black-purple *(A. × prunifolia)*. Though the purple chokeberry is inherently valuable as a native shrub (both on the East Coast and as far west as Michigan), I don't find it as much fun as the other two.

The red chokeberry is a slow-growing, six- to eight-foot upright and informal, suckering shrub. It flowers in May with perfectly pleasant, dense, spiraea-like white clusters lit by red stamens, yet remains largely innocuous till fall, when it turns a vivid—in fact, spectacular—red, as searingly hot as that of the burning bush *(Euonymus alatus)*. The straight species *A. arbutifolia* has been one-upped in the trade by the cultivar 'Brilliantissima', whose autumn leaves range from hues of salmon to scarlet, and whose fruit clusters are both showier and more abundant.

'Brilliantissima' remains splendid after leaf fall, with cherry-red fruits dangling every which way. Before leaf fall, they're so close in color to the shrub's brilliant autumn leaves that they blend into, rather than enhance, the foliage. I'm not saying the cultivar isn't

A. melanocarpa

gorgeous, but the contrast will not take your breath away. For that thrill, plant the black chokeberry, *A. melanocarpa* (syn. *A. arbutifolia* var. *melanocarpa*), whether the unimproved species, the naturally occurring *A. melanocarpa* var. *elata*, or the selection 'Autumn Magic'.

At four to six feet, the black-fruited species is smaller than the red job. It has a thicket-forming tendency and is a bit more colonizing than 'Brilliantissima', but certainly not what you'd call invasive. It, too, has hawthornlike flower clusters in spring, and it makes a good woodland filler through summer, though it must be said that the genus as a whole suffers from ugly ankles (the foliage stops about halfway down the shrub, leaving the stems bare).

Fortunately, *A. melanocarpa* doesn't call much attention to itself until fully dressed, wearing glossy peach, orange, and red-tinted leaves set off by long-stemmed earrings of pendulous black fruit. The fruit/foliage contrast is staggering, and seems to grow in intensity for at least a month, until the foliage drops and the berries linger, waiting to become a hungry bird's last resort.

Callicarpa

DECIDUOUS SHRUB

the facts

BOTANICAL NAME:
Callicarpa

SOUNDS LIKE:
Alan Arka

COMMON NAME:
Beautyberry

TYPE:
Mounding to arching deciduous shrub, 4 to 8 feet
(depending on species)

BASIC NEEDS:
Full to part sun, good
drainage

WORST ENEMY:
Drought, particularly while
getting established

BEST ADVICE:
For better fruiting,
prune out one-third of old
growth each year

It's always been a cheap thrill of mine to watch jaws drop when gardeners see their first purple-berried *Callicarpa*. Even more satisfying, however, is the chance to turn them on to lesser-known, outstanding species of this genus that are rarely seen in Northwest gardens.

But I'm here to report there's only one form of purple beautyberry that truly thrives in temperate climates, the very same one savvy Northwest gardeners already grow: *C. bodinieri* 'Profusion' (syn. *C. bodinieri* var. *giraldii* 'Profusion').

For reasons only guessed at — no doubt related to the weather, and the absence of a long season of heat — none of the other species berry up quite as reliably as this Dutch selection. And since a callicarpa without good fall berries is like a sugar cone without ice cream, why bother having one at all?

So here I sit with a selection of ludicrously delicious, hand-rolled, chocolate-dipped waffle cones wondering how to get you to bite. The best I can do is offer some delectable food for thought.

Bigger berries: *C. americana*, the East Coast native beautyberry, is a tall, dramatically coarse, edge-of-woodlands shrub with violet to magenta fruits nearly three times (three times!) the size of 'Profusion'. When decked out, its branches are completely ringed with glossy baubles, an arresting effect that makes other beautyberries look unreasonably discreet.

Better body: *C. dichotoma*, the purple beautyberry from Japan and China, is easily the most refined and shapeliest species in the genus. It has a horizontal, tiered habit that makes the plant an asset long before it fruits, when cascades of violet berries the size of BBs dance down its arching arms. It reaches four feet by four feet in a season and roots wherever its tips hit the ground.

Brightest color: *C. japonica*, the Japanese beautyberry, is also rounded and horizontal, though not quite as elegant. Its primary asset is its metallic purple fruits, a color just a tad weirder than most, set off dramatically by autumn leaves often touched with pink. The white form, *C. japonica* 'Leucocarpa', is considered quite the treasure, particularly when sited at the edge of woods.

Now I'm not saying that if you live in Oregon City you can't grow any of the above, but you may not be thrilled with the results. Word on the block is, they're duds. And though I might have at first dismissed the overused 'Profusion', I'm now enormously grateful that we in the Northwest have a well-fruiting callicarpa at all.

C. bodinieri 'Profusion'

And what a doer. This Chinese species is in a hurry to grow. It gets off to a very fast start, sending up a strong central leader with side branches that swirl like skirts below its knees. The effect in part shade is lean and gawky—that was my mistake—so give yours full sun. Also, pruning back that dominant leader will help chubby it up early on, but by and large this is a strongly upright, often eight-foot shrub.

'Profusion'—named for its abundant fruit set—is also in a big hurry to berry. A mere twelve-inch stick quickly becomes four feet by three feet and in its first year is splattered with lilac peas. The berries color up in early September on the heels of the plant's sweet but innocuous lavender flowers, which are common to all callicarpa species but only faintly ornamental, and certainly no match for the berries to come.

So who cares if the tireless 'Profusion' is not the most gorgeous beautyberry in cultivation? It's still purple. And that's what the *kallos* (beauty) in the *karpos* (fruit) is all about.

Camellia

BROADLEAF EVERGREEN

the facts

BOTANICAL NAME:
Camellia

SOUNDS LIKE:
Ophelia

TYPE:
Dense, upright, sometimes arching evergreen shrubs, 4 to 9 feet

BASIC NEEDS:
Part shade, evenly moist soils

WORST ENEMY:
Bad drainage; desiccating winds

BEST ADVICE:
If winters are consistently around 0°F to −10°F, stick to *C. oleifera*; fertilize camellias sparingly

Meet Mr. Camellia.

He was a humble Jesuit pharmacist who never knew a self-indulgent moment and died in his early forties serving the poor. No doubt, Georg Josef Kamel would have approved of being associated with a soft-spoken, bashful shrub whose leaves, steeped in boiling water, soothed and sustained millions yet attracted little attention.

You don't mean that slut, the *Camellia*?

Not the one with the swelling buds getting ready to bare all in the New Year, no. I mean the one that blooms in the fall with the single white fragrant flowers, whose leaves have for centuries been the commercial source of tea: *Camellia sinensis*.

The tea camellia was the first named species of this genus; it's the plant from which Earl Grey and all the other choice varieties of tea are made. It's very happy here in the Northwest, where it can grow to a richly textured six-foot plant and can bloom from mid-October through December.

Granted, its flowers are not as prominent as those of other camellias, in part because they're often hidden by leaves. But it's heat- and drought-tolerant, takes full sun, and can be harvested throughout the growing season to make either green or black tea.

Too utilitarian? The nursery trade suspected as much. Let me introduce the gorgeous foliage cultivar, *C. sinensis* 'Rosea'. It has seriously burgundy leaves that hold their blush all summer and pale pink flowers that emerge from deep maroon buds. 'Blushing Maiden' is another pink selection, with single, nodding blossoms and foliage touched with red.

Without a doubt, the most delicate, fragrant, and graceful camellias are the fall bloomers, including *C. oleifera*, the tea-oil camellia, hardy to −10°F. Like *C. sinensis*, it has white, sweet-smelling, single, two-inch flowers, but these are prominently displayed on an open and slightly weeping five- to six-foot shrub. Its loose inclination, plus its skin-smooth, cinnamon bark, make this camellia a particularly good candidate as an espalier.

C. oleifera's extreme hardiness and long-blooming nature have made it a preferred parent for hybridizing. The result is a limitless number of cultivars in a range of flower forms, from single anemone to double peony.

The last word in fall-blooming camellias goes to the species *C. sasanqua;* if I gave it the first word there would be room for nothing else. Like *C. oleifera,* it's fabulously underused and, by November, has little competition in the way of flowering shrubs. It's characterized by fragrant and profuse blooms that do us the great favor of shattering as they age—in contrast to the flowers of the popular Japanese camellia, *C. japonica,* which remain whole and rot on the vine.

C. sasanqua—which can be easily identified by its fuzzy stems—is smaller and more refined in leaf and shape than *C. japonica,* with smaller flowers, though no less diverse in color and form. It comes in, oh, a couple of thousand cultivars.

What have I left out? Only enough to guarantee me execution by the International Camellia Society, whose plant register currently lists over 32,000 named varieties of Mr. Kamel's humble plant.

C. sasanqua

gimme more

Here are a couple of the hardy species, *C. oleiferas:*

'Survivor':
Single white, floriferous; upright

'Twilight Glow':
Single rose; spreading

'Polar Ice':
3.5-inch, white, anemone-like flowers

'Carolina Moonmist':
Pink; selected for dense branching

And for the sluttiest, deepest red:

C. japonica
'Midnight Lover'

Camellia

Carex elata 'Aurea'

the facts

BOTANICAL NAME:
Carex elata 'Aurea' (syn.
C. elata 'Bowles Golden')

SOUNDS LIKE:
Carrots a lot'a

COMMON NAME:
Bowles's golden
sedge or grass

TYPE:
Softly spilling deciduous
grass, 2.5 feet

BASIC NEEDS:
Part shade to full sun;
evenly moist to standing
shallow water

WORST ENEMY:
Dry soil

BEST ADVICE:
You'll get the best color in
full sun, provided it gets
ample water, but expect
some August burn

For want of a penknife, we might never have the sumptuous, golden-haired sedge, *Carex elata* 'Aurea' in our gardens. Fortunately, Edward Augustus Bowles rarely left home without one.

E. A.—as he was later known—was nearing the end of his theology and entomology studies at Cambridge University when, while out hunting moths and caterpillars, he spied a clump of ordinary green sedge that was lightened by a few gold-edged leaves. After a quick drop to his knees to confirm his prey, E. A. whipped out the penknife and, in one swift motion, liberated the golden grass from obscurity and walked (ever modestly) into horticulture's hall of fame.

Bowles's golden sedge is a must-have plant. To see it well grown is an irresistible invitation to tear out anything inferior that marks the edge of a bed or a bend in a path. It spills, shimmers, giggles, and throws light in every direction, reflecting exuberance and confidence on even the most worried, self-deprecating gardener (don't suppose you know any, though).

True, you will need a constant source of summer moisture to grow this golden sedge successfully (perhaps that's not what you're in the mood to hear if your garden's looking puckered and singed)—but we're talking about the chance to drink deeply from the visual equivalent of a bubbling fountain of honey-lemon brew.

Often thirty inches high and wide, *C. elata* 'Aurea' grabs attention easily but doesn't detain it (the art of simplicity), and instead sends the eye journeying out in all directions. It is a specimen plant—a moment, an accent, a breeze—and does wonders to enhance the color and impact of its companions.

And who might they be? No doubt you've got your own notebooks full of great plant combos seen in gardens much nicer than your own. Well, so do I. In the spirit of E. A. Bowles, who was smart enough upon seeing it to grab the gold ring, I invite you to step right up and steal these great golden sedge garden ideas.

From Marietta and Ernie O'Byrne's garden in Eugene, Oregon, we have big, billowing sedges across the path from a huge mound of *Nasturtium* 'Sunshine'. It's a part-shade setting, all the better to see the surrounding gold-leaved *Hypericum* 'Summergold', yellow variegated Hakone grass (*Hakonechloa macra* 'Aureola'), and 'Gold Queen' yew. Nearby, another cauldron of *Carex* simmers among hot-orange candelabra primroses.

In Liz Lair's garden, also in Eugene, *C. elata* 'Aurea' is loudly percussive in full sun in a pot with black mondo grass. The gardener also plays her sedge against the magenta-eyed geraniums 'Ann Folkard' and *G. psilostemon*, and uses it to electrify both blue-leaved hostas and *Corydalis* 'China Blue'.

Other miscellaneous ideas cribbed from my carex-driven wanderings include: an explosive combo with *Ligularia* 'The Rocket', plus purple-leaved *Heuchera* and *Rodgersia;* a refreshing splash alongside late-blooming Japanese iris; a foil for sherbet-orange daylilies; and the centerpiece on a rich cloth of yellow-leaved, blue-flowering *Veronica prostrata* 'Trehane'.

'Knightshayes':
Smaller, to 18 inches, with entirely gold leaves; prefers shade

C. elata 'Aurea'

Carex elata 'Aurea'

Clerodendrum

DECIDUOUS SHRUB

BOTANICAL NAME:
Clerodendrum

SOUNDS LIKE:
Fair addendum

COMMON NAME:
Glorybower (*C. bungei*),
harlequin glorybower
(*C. trichotomum*)

TYPE:
Deciduous, suckering shrub
to 6 feet; open, multiple-
trunked tree, 10 to 20 feet

BASIC NEEDS:
Sun to part shade,
well-drained soil

WORST ENEMY:
Easily offends the olfactory
sense; be careful not to site
C. bungei nose-high

BEST ADVICE:
C. trichotomum will age considerably better either
bought as or trained into a
single-trunked tree

For reasons that remain entirely unclear to me, the plant we now call glorybower was once credited with magical powers. One species was thought to bring good fortune, another to bring bad luck.

Evidently, the eighteenth-century botanist Linnaeus was familiar with this bit of folklore when he gave the genus its scientific name. *Clerodendrum* is from the Greek *kleros*, for "chance" or "destiny," and *dendron*, for "tree."

C. trichotomum

Trouble is, he didn't specify which species bodes ill. But I think I might hazard a guess.

The species *C. bungei* is a five- to six-foot upright shrub with huge, eight-inch heart-shaped leaves that emerge deep burgundy and slowly fade to dark green. Come August, the shrub breaks out in cauliflower-like crowns of deeply saturated, hot pink buds—figure a couple hundred to a head—which then open into bubble gum–pink stars. Arresting from a distance and richly scented close up, these flat-topped flowers bloom sporadically well into September.

What could be bad, right? That's what I said when I saw it in flower. So I planted it on the edge of the patio last fall, despite

fall

134

rumors that it might colonize every inch of available space. Sometime in late April, I began to smell something rancid, a truly gag-me aroma. I figured something was decomposing and waited for it to pass. I'm still waiting.

Yes, it was—and remains—*C. bungei*, specifically its foliage, as stinky as it is ornamental, which is why I can't bring myself to move the shrub. It's just such a looker! Colorful in both leaf and flower, shade-tolerant, and shockingly easy to grow (just try to stop it), it's a dream of a plant that will turn around and bite you if you don't site it carefully. Like downwind, with plenty of room to move.

At the risk of underrating a truly useful shrub—with flowers sweet enough to overwhelm the smell of its leaves—I must now tell you about its better half, the late-blooming *C. trichotomum* (harlequin glorybower), which flowers when precious few woody plants are anything other than green. This is a multiple-trunked, mushroom-topped, one- to two-story-high tree with long, tapered leaves and a flower fragrance you can smell a block away (in this case, that's a good thing).

The star-shaped white blossoms are set off by papery, dusty-rose bracts (actually the calyx of the flower). Pretty impressive. But you ain't seen nuthin' yet. The blossoms then give way to turquoise fruit, set like blue pearls in the belly button of a starfish. How'd the starfish get there? It's the calyx, burst open and dramatically transformed from dusty rose to burning red.

All this blaze of color must explain the "harlequin" half of *C. trichotomum*'s common name. One rub of its leaves and you'll know why it's also called the peanut butter tree. Come to think of it, the leaves on the shrubby *C. bungei* smell a little like peanut butter too— lost in the pantry, three years past its expiration date, the lid ajar. Now that's what I call rotten luck.

Decaisnea fargesii

BOTANICAL NAME:
Decaisnea fargesii

SOUNDS LIKE:
Repays me a Parcheesi tie

COMMON NAME:
Blue bean shrub

TYPE:
Arching and upright
deciduous shrub, 15 feet

BASIC NEEDS:
Sun to part shade

WORST ENEMY:
Nasty, dense soils and
bad pruning; keep plant
open and airy

BEST ADVICE:
Great for a raucous
mixed border

I have before me three fat, blue-stained bean pods the size of a large man's index finger. Their color is somewhere between washed denim and slate. Their two-day-old sagging flesh is eerily humanoid to the touch. They are, in a word, startling.

In the interest of science, I will now pop one of these decadently ripe pods open. Yuchh. (You'd better put this aside for later reading if you're about to eat.) Inside, several dozen black beans are suspended in a liquid that looks like clear phlegm. Truly gross. But you haven't heard the half of it: I am now going to stick my finger in the goop and put it into my mouth.

Hmm. Not bad. Actually, quite sweet. In fact, sort of watermelon-like, in a gelatinous way. Good enough to spread on a little toast, if you could do something about the color. Or, if you had grown up where it was native—such as China's Sichuan province—you might even slurp it straight from the pod.

Introducing *Decaisnea fargesii*. One look at its fall fruit, and you'll never forget the color (I'll understand if you forgo the taste). Trust me, if you've any sense of wonder—or humor—you're going to want this shrub when you find out how easy it is to grow.

D. fargesii comes from a family of plants known largely for its vines, including *Akebia* and *Holboellia*. It's tall, lanky, and arching to about fifteen feet, with blue-green pinnate leaves and an informal effect just this side of tropical (like a better-behaved tree of heaven, *Ailanthus*). Though it's perfectly good-looking, I wouldn't say it's a stand-alone specimen, but its airy presence invites all sorts of underplantings, be they shrubs, perennials, or bulbs.

One of the best uses of this plant I've seen is in a parking strip in Portland, Oregon, where several specimens are spaced along the length of the street, mixed with innumerable—and largely deciduous—companions. The blue bean shrubs are intriguing in spring, with foot-long, drooping panicles of yellow-green flowers, and make

D. fargesii

attractive foliage fillers when the days grow hot. But it's after the parking strip loses its leaves that the iridescent, four-inch fruits come into their glory, suspended in midair like spray-painted sausages, a joke left over from Halloween.

All you need to grow the plant successfully is full sun to part shade, good loamy soil, and a site no more hospitable than a curbside. Then, come next fall, after you've slurped out the fruit's innards, you can plant the magic beans.

Decaisnea fargesii

Helianthus salicifolius

PERENNIAL

the facts

BOTANICAL NAME:
Helianthus salicifolius

SOUNDS LIKE:
He'll eat man thus,
solicit coleus

COMMON NAME:
Willowleaf sunflower

TYPE:
Tall, lightly textured
fall perennial

BASIC NEEDS:
Full sun, dry to average
well-drained soil

WORST ENEMY:
Dry shade

BEST ADVICE:
To avoid floppiness, pinch
back by half in late May

I'll never forget my first assignment as a major league reporter. I was to follow the Darn Yellows Composites (popularly known as the DYCs) as they blew through the American League West en route to the World Series.

In the bottom of the ninth — in what would be a three-game sweep against the German Beardeds — I finally got nervous. One more out and I'd be on my way to the testosterone-drenched locker room. My heart was beating in my stomach as the media flood carried me down the stairs, heading straight for the underbelly of the stadium.

Once in, I could barely see past the reporters surrounding the DYC's superstar, Annual Sunflower. The clichés were flying like winged toasters. "Mr. Sunflower, how long can you stand up to all this pressure?" To which Annual answered, "Mr. Nobody, what could a pissant like you know about pressure?"

Seized by the image of being buried in his spit seed, I thought better of interviewing the egomaniacal Annual, and let my attention wander to an incredibly thin and willowy, six-foot DYC with cordovan-colored eyes. He was fresh from the showers and — just my luck! — already wearing a smartly wrapped towel. His warm, sunny, and unpretentious smile lit the way.

Me: Hey, mind talking for a few minutes?

WS: Happy to. With Annual on the team, the rest of us rarely get a word in edgewise. I'm *Helianthus salicifolius* — my parents were big into Latin — but if you want, you can call me Willowleaf. Willowleaf Sunflower.

Me: Great name. Mine's Ketzel, rhymes with pretzel. Say, Will, you made some great plays from second today. Sheer elegance.

WS: Yeah, I did have a good game. I'm at my best with the sun beating down, even get a buzz from being slightly parched. Guess it keeps me from getting too sloppy, and it sure does keep me lean.

Funny, guys say I look as good in the last game as I did in the first.

Secret could be that come midseason, I cut my size back by half. At least that's how I think of it, stopping myself from getting too heady and focusing my energies on filling out. Also, unlike Annual, I'm a team player, so I hold back my best stuff till the other guys fade. Like till now, pennant time.

H. salicifolius

Me (blushing): And that's some stuff you got, Will. Tell me, do you feel terribly minimized by Annual?

WS: Look, kids need heroes. He's as big as they come. I've got my own following— Kansans, Missourians—folks who root for native sons. I'm also aware of my appeal to the more sophisticated, cerebral fan. Not that I don't turn heads—lady, I'm one hell of a hot dog—but by and large, I'm just a solid, sane, and well-proportioned guy.

Me (blushing even harder): I see that, Will. And given the month, you look positively verdant, as if you've just come in from an April shower. No wonder! You haven't even dressed! Anything else before I leave?

WS: Only this. Size isn't everything. It's how long you can last on the field.

Me (positively crimson): I'll quote you, Will.

And then I left, my notebook full and my heart now sitting on my sleeve. A few weeks later the DYCs lost the pennant to the Midnight Deep Freeze. But I have no doubt they'll be back next summer, with Annual Sunflower showered in unrivaled celebrity, and Willowleaf Sunflower biding his easy time at second, a bright yellow voice in the autumn wind.

Helianthus salicifolius

Humulus lupulus 'Aureus'

DECIDUOUS VINE

the facts

BOTANICAL NAME:
Humulus lupulus 'Aureus'

SOUNDS LIKE:
Hum you must scrupulous glorious

COMMON NAME:
Golden hops

TYPE:
Deciduous vine, to 20 feet

BASIC NEEDS:
Full to part sun; even moisture through summer

WORST ENEMY:
Dry shade

BEST ADVICE:
Play off its color with companion plants to get the most out of this vine

A well-grown golden hops is a vine so full of movement it looks like a frozen waterfall of tumbling, sunlit leaves. On the other hand, a poorly grown one is just a mundane drizzle on a gray day. I ought to know, since I've seen them both—the latter, alas, in my own garden. A bit more sun to bring out the vine's color and a lot more water to give it reason to live, and my yard might now be swaddled in spun gold.

H. lupulus 'Aureus'

Nevertheless, my straggling specimen remains poised for glory. Its lineage promises at least that much, since the species, *Humulus lupulus* — a member of the family Cannabis — is the fruiting vine that begat the brew pub. The golden-leaved cultivar is a nonpalatable ornamental that offers the sentiment (if not the sediment) of our beloved hops and is easily the phonetic equivalent of walking a straight line.

Humulus lupulus 'Aureus' ("Presto! you're an amber ale!") is a botanical incantation not easily deciphered. *Humulus* appears to be the Latinized, medieval word for hops (from humus, or soil, or maybe potted?), with *lupulus* a reference to a small wolf with a habit of climbing over willows. Though the golden hops is hardly predatory, it is a vigorous climber, capable of scaling a deciduous tree in a single season. Always kind to its hosts, however, the vine takes no prisoners, just politely dies back to the ground each year.

If I had to grow *H. lupulus* 'Aureus' again — and I will, if it will have me — I'd mix it with blue clematis and toss it like a feather boa over a snug entry into a lesser part of the garden. I'd train it to scramble up the side of a conifer (preferably a blue one) like a racing stripe, or along the trunk and out the branches of a purple-leaved tree.

I could cover an ugly fence with it (which is what I'd intended, but now the hops is uglier than the fence). I could make a wooden tripod and grow the hops as an ornamental golden tent. I might use its soft light as a ceiling on an arbor, or as a backdrop behind a mixed border. Or I might create a color wall by mixing it with other tinted vines, whether the purple-leaved grape (*Vitis vinifera* 'Purpurea') or the richly mottled, fall-red ivy, *Parthenocissus henryana*.

I offer you these ideas to distract you from doing as I do.

Origanum

"Oregano comes in a jar and, like shoes, is better dried." So says my smart-aleck plantsman friend Uncle Bob. Not much of a veggie gardener, that guy. Fact is, many of us plant geeks get jittery at the thought of growing food in our gardens. Could it be the fear of impending earthiness and family values? Or the guilt of eating our young?

The perennial herb oregano, however, transcends all sociological schisms. The food people get species that taste good, and the geeks get good-looking plants. I'm the wrong person to ask about edible varieties, though I've read that the best cooking oregano is *Origanum heracleoticum* (Greek oregano). But for a handsome and ludicrously long-flowering perennial, the answer is *O. laevigatum*.

What we have here is a low, spreading mat of a plant with frothy bluish-green leaves and long, arching stems that erupt in what appear to be stiff sparklers. Close up, the sparklers are revealed to be made up of tightly packed flowering bracts and absolutely minuscule blooms. These tiny, two-lipped flowers range from pink through mauve to violet purple; after flowering—which could be mid-November—the spent clusters look like doll-sized shafts of wheat.

The straight species *O. laevigatum* has been eclipsed by cultivars and hybrids with bigger and better ornamental traits. Two hit the big time several years ago: 'Herrenhausen', with large clusters of lilac flowers and purple-flushed foliage that deepens color in the fall, and 'Hopley's' (a.k.a. 'Hopley's Purple'), popular among cut-flower growers for its abundant, rich purple blooms. Both reach two feet by two feet and can sprawl, but that's no big deal, you just cut them back in early summer. It won't slow them down.

Or you could try the latest compact kids on the block, including the Dutch introductions 'Rosenkuppel', a one-foot perennial with dark pink flowers and contrasting maroon-purple skirts, and 'Rotkugel', similarly colored but to fifteen inches, with large rounded foliage.

the facts

BOTANICAL NAME:
Origanum

SOUNDS LIKE:
A pig in rum

COMMON NAME:
Oregano

TYPE:
Summer to fall-blooming perennial herb

BASIC NEEDS:
Full sun, good drainage

WORST ENEMY:
Mucky soil

BEST ADVICE:
Cut back once in early summer to avoid legginess

Though certainly not inedible, none of these plants tastes like much. Alice Doyle, herbal maven from Log House Plants of Cottage Grove, Oregon, says that all herbs slow down oil production in their leaves when they're focusing on producing flowers. I did risk eating an *O. laevigatum* flower and could see its merit as a colorful garnish—if one were inclined to chop off its head.

Whether fodder or flower, this member of the mint family is exquisitely easy to grow. Full sun, little water, and fast-draining soil, and, as they say across the ocean, Bob's your uncle. Guy gets around.

O. laevigatum 'Hopley's Purple'

O. laevigatum cultivars:
'Kent Beauty':
  Pink to mauve flowers and rich pink (vs. green) bracts
'Norton Gold':
  Brilliant gold foliage and pink flowers
'Entedank':
  Loose, soft purple panicles; very late blooming

O. vulgare cultivars:
'Variegatum':
  Small leaves etched in creamy white
'Aureum':
  Popular gold-foliage ground cover
'White Anniversary':
  Lime leaves rimmed in white
'Humile':
  Dwarf with purplish winter foliage
'Compactum Nanum':
  Stepping-stone favorite

Origanum

Osmanthus

BROADLEAF EVERGREEN

the facts

BOTANICAL NAME:
Osmanthus

SOUNDS LIKE:
Oz Kansas

COMMON NAMES:
Holly tea olive, false
holly, devilwood

TYPE:
Dense, blocky, fall-to-spring-
blooming, broadleaf ever-
green, 5 to 25 feet

BASIC NEEDS:
Sun to partial shade

WORST ENEMY:
Undue optimism; cold har-
diness varies with species,
so be realistic

BEST ADVICE:
A superb option
for a sweet-smelling
evergreen hedge

We gardeners have a sense of smell that's long on nuance. But we're short on words to describe fragrance, so we borrow from the language of food. Flowers smell like oranges, honey, cinnamon, and vanilla. Bazooka and Juicy Fruit gum. Or, in the case of *Osmanthus,* all of the above—with a little suntan lotion rubbed in.

Having long dismissed osmanthus as a utilitarian hedge plant, I am now besotted with its possibilities, both as a specimen and as a source of heady aroma anywhere from September into May. At least eight distinct species deserve profiles unto themselves, but I suspect few of us have attention spans that could take all that, since—despite appreciable differences in plant size and leaf shape—we are talking a fairly basic hollylike evergreen with inconspicuous white flowers.

Fragrance, as I've said, is a far more complex matter, and the fall-blooming species *O. fragrans,* the fragrant tea olive, sets the standard. It makes a rather vast, twenty- to thirty-foot hunk of deep, dark green; that is, if we can successfully grow it. Turns out *O. fragrans* needs serious coddling against desiccating winter winds. Worse yet, according to Portland, Oregon, plantsman Paul Bonine—who's learned by losing them—Northwest summers are often neither long nor hot enough for *O. fragrans* to lignify, that is, to develop wood. Consequently, an unestablished shrub is essentially naked when winter hits; without a thermal, woody layer, it succumbs at about 20°F.

On the other hand, if you're lucky enough to get hold of the showy orange form 'Aurantiacus' (syn. *O. fragrans* f. *aurantiacus*), I'd risk it. Word is it's slightly more hardy, and my, what a looker. Site it in a sheltered, sunny position that takes full advantage of its pastel flowers and autumnal perfume.

The species Bonine thinks should be "the denim of plants in western Oregon" is *O. heterophyllus,* a.k.a. false holly. Fabulously adapted to heavy clay and drought, intensely disliked by deer,

O. *heterophyllus* cultivars come dense and prickly, smooth-edged and shiny, flecked with colors or rimmed with creamy white. The darling these days is 'Goshiki', whose name means "five colors" in Japanese. It's a nicely fragrant, variegated little guy (to five feet), blotched and streaked with yellow, which can be stuffed in a hot, sunny border or used to illuminate part shade.

Another small stunner is 'Sasaba', which "brings squeals and squeaks of delight" to all who see it in the Washington state garden of Heronswood Nursery co-owner Dan Hinkley. It's a choice introduction only ten years old, whose Japanese name is a reference to its linear, bamboolike leaves.

'Sasaba' is for the collector, but this one's for everyone else: O. *heterophyllus* 'Purpureus', so dependably hardy it can be grown as a hedge where temperatures drop to –10°F, and so stunning in leaf it can hold its own as a mixed-border specimen. As its name suggests, this fast-growing cultivar has leaves—and stems—that emerge a glorious, deep, dark purple, eventually fading to a lustrous green. It can be whacked back or left to grow its full one-and-a-half-story height, and asks only full sun to glow.

Notice that I've moved my emphasis on fragrance to foliage, which is not to say the previous cultivars don't smell sweet. But for bone hardiness and apricot sweetness, get a load of the hybrid, O. × *fortunei* 'San Jose'. It has dramatically serrated leaves and an upright habit that lends itself to hedging, plus a sublime scent that will perfume a cold, drizzly day with memories of summer and promises of spring.

O. *heterophyllus* 'Goshiki'

gimme more

More O. *heterophyllus* cultivars:

'Aureomarginata':
Variegated with yellow margins

'Gulftide':
Glossy, slightly twisted, spiny leaves; to 8 feet or prune as hedge

'Rotundifolius':
Smooth-edged, undulate leaves; 3-foot-by-4-foot mound

'Variegatus':
Margins creamy white; amazingly durable and long-lived

Osmanthus

Oxydendrum arboreum

DECIDUOUS TREE

the facts

BOTANICAL NAME:
Oxydendrum arboreum

SOUNDS LIKE:
Moxie men dumb are
boring them

COMMON NAMES:
Sourwood, lily of the
valley tree

TYPE:
Upright, architectural, deciduous tree, 20 to 50 feet

BASIC NEEDS:
Part shade to full sun
(sun for best flowering/fall
color); good drainage,
even moisture

WORST ENEMY:
Dry shade

BEST ADVICE:
This guy really suffers in
poorly drained clay soil; take
some care finding the right
well-drained site

I'm just back from walking—or should I say flying?—through Port-land's Hoyt Arboretum. What might have been a leisurely stroll became a forced march, thanks to the hopped-up beagle pulling on the lead (he was a new model, not quite yet broken in). I had gone to Hoyt to see a sourwood tree, which I was told I'd find on the Wildwood Trail.

So five minutes into the walk, doing a fast scan across all manner of leafy greens, I found myself thinking: Yeah, right, how am I going to find a couple of lousy trees in the middle of all this generic vegetation? I snickered at my own smug confidence, thinking I knew enough about plant ID to spot *Oxydendrum arboreum* at a few hundred paces.

By the time I got to the intersection of the Wildwood and Cherry trails, young Jimmy had just about freed my arm from its socket. I cursed myself for not bringing along a good tree book. I was ready to about-face and let him drag me home when I noticed an impos-ing shape in the distance. My nagging self shut up fast once we'd confirmed it was an oxydendrum, a tree too poised and polished to overlook, even in the most like-minded crowd.

The fall color hadn't quite happened yet, but the tree's leathery, slightly glossy foliage was infused with enough mahogany to suggest what would soon follow: wine-red notes lightened by the tinkling of pink and lavender with a sporadic smattering of yellow. All this plus summer's leftover flower stems at the end of each branch, French-polished fingernails set off by ruffle-sleeved leaves.

Though no two *O. arboreum* specimens are precisely alike—in fact, their irregularity is a given—this tree had two straight, lean trunks offset by arms of downward-curving foliage. All the better to set off the spent flower fingers, which reached down, then up at the tips. The entire plant was in motion even while still, reminiscent of *Pieris japonica* covered in its spring filigree. (I used to think of the sourwood as pieris-on-a-stick.)

All sourwoods are extremely slow-growing, that is, a foot a year. Though they are capable of becoming several stories tall, it's likely you'll have moved before that happens. Still, whether as street trees or garden specimens, their formal shape and forgiving manner make them exceptional plants even when young, asking only sun, good soil, and supplemental summer water to flower heavily in summer and blush brilliantly in fall.

O. arboreum

I managed about fifteen minutes of note-taking before my higher-maintenance companion heard the fast-approaching clink of dog tags. We were off like a shot. By then, the wind had picked up, the sky had darkened, and the season was falling fast around me. As we whizzed back to the car, we passed a trio of sourwoods I'd completely missed on our way in. But that was when I'd been distracted by my own chatter, instead of letting the tree speak for itself.

Oxydendrum arboreum

Persicaria

PERENNIAL

Some pages back, I stepped into a nomenclatural bottomless pit called *Fallopia*. The genus was a splinter group—surgically removed by botanists—from what used to be a more encompassing genus, *Polygonum*.

Well, I must have been brain-dead when I decided to write about the fleeceflower, *Persicaria*, because here I am again, mucking around in all this cocka-mamie nomenclature, driven by a compulsive need to get things right at the risk of boring you to tears.

Persicaria was also a splinter group from the brittle *Polygonum*, but no sooner did we make that bed than the genus *Tovara* wanted to crawl in. Weeping big tears over the exile from her beloved family, *Tovara virginiana* had been renamed *Persicaria filiformis* and was now anxiously seeking permanent asylum in the fleeceflower camp.

What to do? Throw the bolt, turn the lock! How else can we possibly get to know any of the persicarias, if the family's size obscures one and all? Therein lies my excuse for writing about one iddy-biddy species and, in particular, the brightest jewel in its crown.

I'm talking about that comet of crimson, *P. amplexicaule* 'Firetail',

P. amplexicaule 'Firetail'

BOTANICAL NAME:
Persicaria

SOUNDS LIKE:
Curse a carrier

COMMON NAME:
Fleeceflower

TYPE:
Fall-blooming perennial

BASIC NEEDS:
Full sun, even moisture

WORST ENEMY:
Dry shade

BEST ADVICE:
Destined to be planted with ornamental grasses

with deep-red flower spikes that head skyward from a stocky green launch pad, three feet and pocket change high. It's a perennial that became popular in the early '90s, right about the time of that egocentric concoction called "the New American Garden"—since maligned for its grandiose title, but still a legit concept with all the comforts of home.

'Firetail' fit right into this uniquely American style (stolen lock, stock, and seed head from Germany, I might add): breezy yet multifaceted, richly textured but not fussy, and above all, fluid in the wind. The key to its composition came down to the cascading foliage and giddy plumes of any and all ornamental grasses.

Not surprisingly, in almost every encounter I've had with 'Firetail', the ornamental grass *Miscanthus* is blooming nearby. This voluptuous companion turns the crimson comet into a kinetic rendering of autumn, to which you might then add the blackened seed heads of *Monarda*, the long licks of blue *Salvia*, or the somber weight of purple-leaved smokebush *(Cotinus coggygria)* to keep things grounded.

In addition to its striking flowers, 'Firetail' has a forceful texture, with big, heart-shaped leaves that greedily grasp their stems (the species name, *amplexicaule*, translates as "clasping leaves"). Bold, yes, but not the kind of foliage that deserves pride of place in the garden. If I might cut to the chase, this is a filler plant, best grown without censure, or planted in mass.

If you're working in a small space and need groundcover, read all about it in the "gimme more" list, where I overcome my xenophobia about those exiled yearning masses and throw the doors open to all.

gimme more

P. affinis:
Vigorous, low-growing species with late spring to fall flowers and colorful fall foliage; great for small gardens; 15 inches. Cultivars include:

'Border Jewel':
Creamy white flowers with red calyces; 4 inches

'Darjeeling Red':
Deep red flowers that fade to pink

'Dimity':
Long-blooming pink spikes turning red with age

P. filiformis (syn. Tovara virginiana):
Aggressive groundcover, grown for three-season foliage; prefers evenly moist soil, part shade; 2 feet by *look out!*

'Painter's Palette':
Green with maroon markings, yellow patches, deep pink tints

'Variegata':
Green with gorgeous ivory mottling

Pistacia chinensis

DECIDUOUS TREE

Plant hunter Ernest Henry Wilson—better known as E. H.—was on his third trip to China when he came across *Pistacia chinensis*. It wasn't exactly high on his list. About that same time in 1908, he'd received appalling news from his benefactor, the Arnold Arboretum: The eighteen thousand lily bulbs he'd shipped from Ichang to Boston had rotted en route.

"Knocked all of a heap" by the news, Wilson seems to have made a quick recovery, and set about digging up and sending back twenty-five thousand more (no comment). He also continued the work that made him famous—introducing astonishing new plants from the Far East—conquests that had so far included *Acer griseum,* the paperbark maple, and *Kolkwitzia amabilis,* the beautybush. This trip, he bagged the Chinese pistache.

It's possible E. H. had already seen a rare specimen of pistacia growing at Kew Gardens, or perhaps his first glimpse of the plant came in the wild. In either case, having witnessed its wondrous fall color, you better believe he snatched seed and sent it home.

P. chinensis is a member of the family *Anacardiaceae,* which includes the smoke tree, *Cotinus,* and the sumac, *Rhus.* Not a bad pedigree if you're looking for a heart-stopping autumnal blaze. What makes this tree particularly valuable in my Northwest neck of the woods is that it doesn't need cold temperatures to trip its trigger, and will turn kaleidoscopic colors despite prolonged heat and a dearth of summer rain (ordinarily, a parched August/September will wreak havoc with fall color).

In addition to its showy, sumaclike plumage, the Chinese pistache is a superb choice for tough urban sites. It'll stand up to pollution, drought, lousy soil, or restricted root space and still grow into an impressive, spreading, twenty- to thirty-five foot tree (capable of fifty feet). Its spring flowers aren't much, but the peppercorn-sized fruits on the female trees can be showy, maturing from yellow

P. chinensis

P. vera:
The true pistachio is a small bushy tree with handsome glaucous leaves. It's hardy to 10°F in the hottest spot in the garden, but requires a long, hot summer and both male and female plants to fruit.

to red to metallic blue if they haven't first gone to the birds. You wouldn't want to eat them anyway, since this is not the edible pistachio tree (though *P. chinensis* is used as an understock for growing *P. vera,* the real nut).

Who knows why the Chinese pistache is conspicuously absent as a street tree in the Northwest? It's certainly not difficult to find in the trade. Perhaps the reason's been no more than an error in the *Sunset Western Garden Book* (since rectified), which insisted the tree was not reliably hardy in the Northwest. In any event, expect to see more of it, thanks to the efforts of indefatigable hortheads, now lobbying hard to get this once-Chinese rarity into the urban mainstream.

Pistacia chinensis

Rhus typhina

DECIDUOUS SHRUB

BOTANICAL NAME:
Rhus typhina

SOUNDS LIKE:
Goose by Lena

COMMON NAME:
Sumac

TYPE:
Multistemmed, spreading,
deciduous shrubs with outstanding fall color;
5 to 25 feet

BASIC NEEDS:
Light and air; full sun for
best foliage show

WORST ENEMY:
Its own greed

BEST ADVICE:
If you're buying the cutleaf
sumac, make sure it's the
staghorn species, *R. typhina*;
there's also an *R. glabra*
'Laciniata', but you won't get
the velveteen antlers

Meet the Sumacs: Staghorn, Shining, and Smooth. "Like a great, unruly mob," writes Carol Ottesen in *The Native Plant Primer.* "Colonizing, suckering, rampant, spreading," writes Michael Dirr in his *Hardy Trees and Shrubs.*

And it's a good thing this mob's on the rampage. Otherwise, the entire country would be bereft of the most brilliant fall foliage that plays across the U.S.A. Massachusetts is blazing with staghorn, *R. typhina*; Minnesota's shining with *R. copallina*; and in the Pacific Northwest, west of the Cascade Range, the smooth stems of *R. glabra* hold some of the best native leaf color around.

Better yet, what an enormous relief to be able to enjoy these three galloping sumacs at a distance, not only allowing us to sleep soundly without fear of invasion, but leaving us room in our gardens to cavort with less rampant *Rhus* species.

Which is not to say the deeply dissected *R. typhina* 'Laciniata' isn't a landgrabber at heart, but it's manageable and well worth the effort. I'm crazy about this shrub. It's a blaze of yellows and oranges in autumn, a velveteen spread of antlers tipped by crimson fruit in winter, and a dramatic yet fine-textured foliage plant both spring and summer. With sun and soil, the cutleaf sumac is impossible not to grow well.

R. typhina 'Laciniata'

Containing its spread is a thankless task that will cost you one great shrub silhouette, so rather than aggravate yourself, give 'Laciniata' a dramatic setting and as much horizontal space as you can—at least six feet.

Same goes for the Chinese sumac, *R. chinensis,* and its selected form 'September Beauty', probably the only sumac grown for its bloom. By late summer, this twenty-foot-high by who- knows-how-wide shrub appears to explode in huge ivory-white asterisks—we're talking foot-wide flower panicles reminiscent of frizzed-out astilbe—which last for several weeks. It has bright green foliage that turns orange-red in autumn, but the flowers set this one apart.

If your space is limited, do I have a little rhus for you: desert or littleleaf sumac *(R. microphylla).* It's a Southwest native with minuscule foliage on a three- to five-foot plant with showy orange summer berries, good fall color, and dense, zigzagging stems. Portland horticulturist Sean Hogan has collected several clones in New Mexico and loves to use *R. microphylla* in his dry border.

Hogan considers it the demure southern cousin of the coarser threeleaf sumac, *R. trilobata,* also known as skunkbush. Despite its common name, it's not that much more pungent than the fragrant sumac, *R. aromatica,* with foliage that smells like mouthwash when crushed. A particularly useful dwarf form of fragrant sumac called 'Gro-Low' lends itself to massing as a groundcover and tolerates some shade.

We do have a renowned native sumac, yes sir, right here in western Oregon. If you've ever run into it, you'll probably never do so again. It turns a stupendous scarlet in the fall, but you don't want it in your garden. It's named for its lobed foliage, which might make you think it's an oak. Botanists call it *Toxicodendron diversilobum;* diehards still refer to it as *Rhus diversiloba.* The rest of us call it trouble: poison oak.

Rhus typhina

Salvia guaranitica

PERENNIAL

the facts

BOTANICAL NAME:
Salvia guaranitica

SOUNDS LIKE:
Salvia swore, admit it, suh!

COMMON NAME:
Anise-scented sage

TYPE:
Fall-blooming tender
perennial

BASIC NEEDS:
Full sun, amended soil, good
drainage

WORST ENEMY:
Single-digit temperatures

BEST ADVICE:
Cut back in June to avoid
legginess, and stand by for
November blooms

Autumn is stunningly sentimental. And so simple. Throw the bleached kindling of an ornamental grass onto a waiting bonfire of deciduous shrubs, toss in a six-foot spark of anise-scented sage, then stand back and warm your cheeks in the glow.

You could read by the electric blue light cast by the flowers of *Salvia guaranitica,* a sage native to South America and introduced to cultivation at least one hundred fifty years ago. Its common name, anise-scented sage, is a reference to the culinary freshness of its bruised leaves. The species stands out because of its inextinguishable flowering flames, which flicker high above the foliage and add bolts of brilliance to the wild autumnal garden.

Though flower color varies according to cultivar, this is what you get with every *S. guaranitica*: At least four to six feet of extreme upright behavior culminating in an eight- to ten-inch spike, stacked with loud-mouthed, two-lipped, two-inch flowers that begin chatting pleasantly in summer and become a great chorus by fall. Like those of all salvias, the flowers' lips are of unequal length and protrude from a megaphone-like device known as the calyx (actually an outer ring of sepals), often colored a simple green but sometimes quite dramatic.

In the case of *S. guaranitica* 'Omaha Gold', you'll see a moody midnight calyx announcing cobalt blue flowers, set off to great effect by softly variegated foliage. The two-tone, green-on-green leaves are subtle enough to appeal to even the nonvariegated types among you, and in the right light they seem to cast complicated shadows on a species that is otherwise unastonishing until it blooms.

I'm not knocking the green forms of the anise-scented sage — their minty leaves are pleasantly heart-shaped, their habit easy to live with, and their flowers spectacular — but 'Omaha Gold' mixed with any foliage plant named 'Aurea' earns its keep long before the big show (which can last until December if there's no killing frost).

Not that you're looking at much overhead, spring through summer, just full sun, good soil and drainage, and the occasional deep drink (every week or ten days during rainless months should do the trick). 'Omaha Gold' can top out at eight feet—no staking required—but for a bushier plant, you may want to cut it back in June. Your only aggravation is likely to be the plant's hardiness (10°F if you're inclined to play it safe, zero if you're in it for the fun). Fortunately, the flowering sages are incredibly easy to grow from September cuttings, so you can always take out insurance. Either that or skip a few four-inch pots of cosmos next spring and plan ahead for the cool blue flames of fall.

S. guaranitica 'Omaha Gold'

The straight species, *S. guarantica,* tends to make bigger clumps and flowers more prolifically. Its color is an intense indigo blue, 5 feet by 3 feet, and it comes in these flavors:

'Argentine Skies':
Light electric blue
'Black and Blue':
Black calyx, rich blue flowers
'Purple Majesty'
(actually a hybrid): Royal purple, larger flowers than most

Schizostylis

BULBOUS PLANT

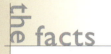
the facts

Faster-spreading than an *Acidanthera,* more powerful than an autumn crocus, able to leap through seasons at a time. Is it an iris? Is it a gladiolus?

No! It's *Schizostylis!*

Named for the split or distinctly branching appearance of the plant's *style*—the elongated part of the pistil—the genus *Schizostylis* is an easy read. Unlike its more complicated relatives *Iris* and *Crocus,* it contains just one species, *S. coccinea* (syn. *S. pauciflora*), which does come in a small range of colors, but all with the same unmistakable bloom.

Native to South Africa, Natal, and Swaziland, the so-called kaffir lily—a rather derogatory, colonial name—is usually found growing along river and stream banks, where its roots are almost constantly in water. Yet it's gloriously adaptable even in the suburban wilds of Portland, Oregon, proving that despite its tropical inclinations, the scarlet river lily is a robust and hardy plant.

Schizostylis is a rhizome that forms extensive patches of narrow, grasslike leaves in upright, arching clumps. The flower stalks rise out of the foliage, up to two and a half feet high, with slender buds that taper like ink brushes. Of the six to ten buds per stem, at least two are usually open at one time: starry, scarlet flowers reminiscent of another South African native, freesia.

Unlike freesia, though, schizostylis is not fragrant, nor is it remotely as tender. All this piece-of-cake plant needs to thrive is ample sun, reasonable drainage, and summer water. Keep it evenly moist from May through August, and the payoff comes in September, when schizostylis begins to flower in shades of soft pink through fire red. Prone to confusion, it may be December — or quite possibly May — before it remembers to stop.

S. coccinea 'Major'

gimme more

S. coccinea cultivars:
'Alba':
  White with a whiff of pink, slightly less vigorous
'Big Mama':
  Pink, larger flower
'Cherry Red':
  Showy lipstick red, seen blooming in December
'Major':
  Larger flower, also seen in December
'Mrs. Hegarty':
  Clear to rose pink
'Oregon Sunset':
  Robust, watermelon red
'Sunrise':
  Rich pink with twisting flower stems

Schizostylis

Solidago

PERENNIAL

BOTANICAL NAME:
Solidago

SOUNDS LIKE:
How'd your day go

COMMON NAME:
Goldenrod

TYPE:
Late summer or fall-
blooming yellow perennial

BASIC NEEDS:
Sun and soil

WORST ENEMY:
Itself, it seems; aggressive
species have given the
genus a bad name

BEST ADVICE:
Choose the appropriate
variety for your site; that is,
don't plant a species that
wants to be naturalized
in a small, select border

Poor goldenrod! Every blessed word written about this North American native begins with an apology. The litany goes something like this:

Yes, it's common along roadsides, but that doesn't make it a weed. Sure, it's incredibly easy to grow, but that doesn't cheapen its virtue. True, its foliage can be coarse and ragged, but there's just nothing else like it in flower. And no, goldenrod does *not* cause hay fever. The real culprit is ragweed, a less-conspicuous plant that blooms at the same time.

Now that we've determined what *Solidago* isn't, consider without apology what it is:

Late-blooming. Beginning mid-August and lasting into October, the primary yellows of this aster family member hit the same key introduced by the daffodils of spring and the daylilies of high summer. Consider them the last bold, brash sound of color before the subtle (I'll say) sounds of November.

Undemanding. That is, unless you think soil and sun are a lot to ask.

Well socialized. Though at its best among similarly easygoing, late-season celebrants, goldenrod's got enough hats to crash quite a number of garden parties.

Solidago rugosa 'Fireworks' is a rowdy mass of yellow wands, a four- to five-foot plant that prefers the company of tall asters and giant grasses. *S. sphacelata* 'Golden Fleece' offers the same jolt but on a compact, bubbling two-foot-by-one-foot form. Smaller still is an exciting new dwarf species, *S. roanensis* var. *monticola,* just introduced by Niche Gardens in Chapel Hill, North Carolina, for serious front-of-the-border fun.

S. canadensis 'Lightning Rod'

A number of species dislike pampering and do better when naturalized. *S. sempervirens,* the seaside goldenrod, flops in rich garden soil, but give it a landscape that's hot, harsh, and sandy and the plant is more than just pretty: its aggressive root system can help mitigate erosion. *S. rigida,* topped with domed clusters of showy flowers, is lovely in bud, bloom, and seed and incredibly useful in difficult soils, damp to bone-dry.

S. canadensis, a species native to Oregon west of the Cascades, may be a bit vulgar for the cultivated gardener, but the popular, knee-high 'Crown of Rays' wears a Hedda Hopper topping of brilliant yellow on tidy green foliage. Other dwarf goldenrods are easily identifiable by their chokingly sweet names; whether 'Golden Baby', 'Golden Wings', or 'Peter Pan', expect good manners if not a flamboyant show.

Not long ago a gold-and-green-leaved variegated sport of the species showed up at Collector's Nursery in Battle Ground, Washington. The owners named it 'Lightning Rod' and now sell this bushy, four-foot specimen, not easily found in the trade, through their mail-order catalog. They also offer the hot new cultivar 'Gold Spangles', boldly splashed with color and only two to three feet tall.

I'd be remiss if I didn't warn you that some goldenrods will self-seed, get piggy, and run like thieves. Even a named cultivar, for instance the beautiful 'Fireworks', can get a little hot to handle. A sure way to avoid disaster is to err on the cautious side and start with just one plant. No apology needed; next year, just buy a couple more.

gimme more

What happens when you cross a goldenrod with an aster?

You get the bigeneric hybrid, **x Solidaster.** Honest! Though more of a weaver than an upright perennial, this natural cross makes a great cut flower. Look for **x S. luteus,** with canary-yellow flowers on 30-inch stems, and 'Lemore', a delicious pale lemon variety.

Solidago

Tricyrtis

WOODLAND PERENNIAL

the facts

In the category of unfathomable mysteries, I nominate the flower of *Tricyrtis formosana* 'Samurai'. To even begin unraveling this one, you'll need to observe this gem from a distance of no more than six inches from your face (adjust distance according to age).

Its style (as in a plant's sexual parts) looks like a giraffe's neck, its anthers look like the eyes on a slug, its stamens arch like show-erheads, and its six differently shaded petals (actually tepals) alter-nate like men and women at a dinner table. This whole surrealistic fantasy stands on three pairs of green rubber boots (swollen spurs that are part of the petals), which, kicked three times, reveal the source of the plant's Latin name: *tri,* meaning three, and *kyrtos,* meaning humped.

Unless massed and displayed prominently—up front and center where you're inclined to sit and gaze into its face—the blossom of *T. formosana* 'Samurai' is easy to miss in the garden (though its gold-edged foliage does look good for months). But one close encounter with its amethystine reflection and you'll soon see why this selec-tion—if not the entire genus—is among today's trendiest plants.

Its subtlety has snob appeal (what you call your basic "connois-seur plant"). Add bonus points for flowering both late and in shade. Then there's the unsung-genus factor, a de facto status for any trendy plant. Only a decade ago, if you wanted a toad lily, you could find *T. hirta* and little else. Today, hybridizers from Oregon, Ger-many, and Japan are hurriedly breeding them for bigger flowers and better habits; at last count, more than forty distinct selections were carried by nurseries.

Tricyrtis is native to Korea, Japan, China, even the Philippines (botanical name, *T. imeldae.* Must be the boots.). All are arching clumps of two- to three-foot woodland plants that typically bloom mid-August to October, in flower colors ranging from yellow and white to purple-flecked. Leaves may be bright gold, glossy green, or

T. formosana 'Samurai'

subtly varie-
gated, and cul-
ture is easy: even
moisture and light
shade, rarely sun.

The toad lily is an
instant attention-getter once
you mention its common name.
Unfortunately, the truth is less than
enchanting, having nothing to do with
bewitched princes exiled on floating
pads. Instead, the name has been traced
to the Philippine species, *T. imeldae*, which
grows in a region that is home to the Tasaday tribe. Tasaday hunters would crush the
plant's many parts and leave the juice on
their hands because the scent attracted frogs
and the sticky juice made the frogs less slip-
pery to catch.

Granted, this does little to explain the toad
or the lily, but it does make a much nicer nickname than "suckered frog."

gimme**more**

**PURPLE AND WHITE
FLOWERS**
T. affinis:
Bowl-shaped 1-inch flow-
ers with purple spots

T. hirta 'Miyazaki':
Heavy flowering along
arching stems

T. 'Tojen' (syn. 'Togen'):
Large unspotted laven-
der flowers: bold, shiny
green foliage

WHITE FLOWERS
T. hirta 'White Towers':
Felted, arching stems
of flowers

T. 'Empress':
Extra-wide flowers with
almost spidery petals

T. 'Shirohototogisu':
Prolific display in late
summer

YELLOW FLOWERS
T. macranthopsis:
2-inch waxy, drooping
yellow bells; no sun

VARIEGATED LEAVES
T. affinis 'Tricolor':
Green-, pink-, and white-
swirled leaves with
yellow flowers

T. 'Lemon Lime':
Gold and green leaves with
lavender-banded flowers

Tricyrtis

Vitis

DECIDUOUS VINE

the facts

BOTANICAL NAME:
Vitis

SOUNDS LIKE:
Tightest

COMMON NAME:
Ornamental grape vine

TYPE:
Deciduous vine,
10 to 40 feet

BASIC NEEDS:
Sun to part shade, average
moisture

WORST ENEMY:
Shade if you're after purple
leaves (needs sun)

BEST ADVICE:
Think of the purple-
leaved and variegated
grapevines as *Clematis*; mingle them up and through
larger plants

It's time to bash the prevailing myth that September is the start of russet gold. Most leaves wouldn't dream of falling just yet, and the Japanese maple show is a good four to six weeks away. Gardens are still swimming in rich blue monks-hoods, salmon *Phygelius*, fragrant white tobacco, plus the plum pur-ples best sampled on the claret vine.

Vitis vinifera 'Purpurea' has deeply lobed leaves that emerge with an almost leaden tint. Neither green nor yet purple, they are instantly ornamental, an effect enhanced by a whitish down coat that eventually fades. If planted in full sun, the leaves ripen to a rich, muted burgundy by summer—a color not so much dazzling as moody—which can add enormous depth to gid-dier plants such as the weeping silver-leaved pear.

The vine itself is at its most punch-drunk in autumn, as it ends life in a blaze of scarlet, a fabulous contrast with its own near-black grapes. These are tiny, tightly clustered fruits, each one the size of a pencil eraser, with a taste that some find unpleasant but others describe as simply not sweet.

Incomparably less aggressive than most grapevines, maxing out at ten feet, 'Purpurea' is neck and neck out of the chute with the incredibly handsome *V. vinifera* 'Variegata'. Its lightly spattered lime-green foliage looks awfully pretty as it unfurls, the undersides of the leaves tinged pink.

V. vinifera 'Purpurea'

'Variegata' needs part shade and more water than its purple counterpart. Diana Ballantyne of Oregon Trail Gardens in Boring, Oregon, says she has yet to see a fully mature specimen, but she imagines it will also top out at ten feet, and hears that its fruit is edible. She likes the way it looks with purple, and recommends using it mixed in with a purple-flowered clematis or climbing through a dark-leaved smokebush. For fall color, expect the inevitable russet gold.

Lastly, an ornamental grape that is a true folial wonder, even without stripes, splashes, or moody leaves: *V. coignetiae* is native to the mountain forests of northern Japan, where it has been described as covering trees from base to summit with a gorgeous autumn mantle. Its dark and leathery individual leaves—a foot long!—have a thick felt undercoating in colors ranging from rust to vanilla. They make a wonderful roof (if given seriously strong support) all summer, and turn all tones of crimson in fall.

gimme**more**

V. californica **'Roger's Red':**
A selected form of a California species. With ample, even moisture, it turns a hot fall color; fruit is for the birds.

Vitis

163

winter

Abies koreana

the facts

BOTANICAL NAME:
Abies koreana

SOUNDS LIKE:
Rabies Laurie Anna

COMMON NAME:
Korean fir

TYPE:
Large, cone-shaped conifer;
to 30 feet

BASIC NEEDS:
Full sun and good drainage

WORST ENEMY:
Muck and shade

BEST ADVICE:
This is a slow-growing,
long-haul landscape tree

It's no easy task for a Bat Mitzvah girl to recommend a living Christmas tree. I've never had one, never bought one, and only recall decorating two. But if the opportunity came along, I'd do as many of you do and buy something I could integrate into the garden. So, as one plant nerd to another, here's my choice for a small recyclable conifer: *Abies koreana*.

At maturity (figure a couple of decades, since this is a slow grower), the Korean fir can be expected to reach an average of thirty feet. It needs only sun, good drainage, and time in order to thrive. Its habit, though pyramidal, is looser and more layered than that of our grand fir (*A. grandis*), giving it an indulgent, luxurious feel. Close up, its needles are short and chubby, glossy green on top and silver-lined below.

Sounds pretty generic, you say? What's the big deal? Cones, I answer. Fat dollops at least as profuse as raindrops, each one an unimaginable shade of Tootsie Pop purple. From a distance they read like flowers—all the more amazing when you find out they're really composed of dry, woody scales.

These perky, promiscuous ornaments are in such a hurry they're already showing off when the young trees are barely knee-high. But before you get carried away with visions of these sugarplums, you need to know that firs develop cones only in late spring. The good news, of course, is what you then can look forward to, long after the (biodegradable) tinsel has turned to mulch.

Reasonably mature Korean firs are big sellers—and include the narrow-spired, heavily coned 'Starker's Dwarf', which tops out at about six feet; 'Silberlocke' (syn. 'Horstmann's Silberlocke'), with silver-backed needles that curve up and twist around the stem; and 'Aurea', a slow-growing, golden-yellow four-footer. Because of unpredictable nursery stampedes, growers are sometimes caught short. I don't say this to discourage you, only to suggest that you prepare to settle for a somewhat smaller tree than the one you see in your mind's eye—destined, nonetheless, to be a stirring Christmas memory with all the promise of a candy-colored spring.

Tips for keeping your live Christmas tree alive:

◼ Move it into the garage for three or four days, and water well before bringing it into the house.

◼ Keep it inside for no longer than a week, and keep it away from direct heat.

◼ If necessary, water further by placing ice on top of the soil.

◼ Put it back in the garage to acclimate it for life outside. A week or two will do.

◼ After planting, be sure the tree does not dry out.

◼ Should your climate prohibit winter planting, remember to prepare the hole in fall.

A. koreana

Abies koreana

Arbutus menziesii

BROADLEAF EVERGREEN

the facts

BOTANICAL NAME:
Arbutus menziesii

SOUNDS LIKE:
Are you Tess,
Ken Kesey I

COMMON NAME:
Pacific madrone

TYPE:
Large, spreading,
broadleaf evergreen tree, 30
feet and up

BASIC NEEDS:
Full sun; lean, fast-
draining soil

WORST ENEMY:
Heavy clay soil,
overindulgent gardeners

BEST ADVICE:
Water conscientiously until
established, then do not
disturb; trees grown from
seed are your best bet if
you're thinking grove

I have no need to embarrass myself waxing eloquent over our native madrone. The besotted writer Bret Harte beat me to it in his poem, "Madrono":

> Captain of the Western wood,
> Thou that apest Robin Hood!
> Green above thy scarlet hose,
> How thy velvet mantle shows;
> Never tree like thee arrayed,
> O thou gallant of the glade!

It gets worse, but I now understand why. The species invites hyperbole. *Arbutus menziesii* is not just a tree, it's a sentient creature, with curative powers that are drawn from the very soul of the Pacific Northwest.

Hey, this isn't opinion. This is folklore. Hasn't anyone ever told you to hug a madrone? I was encouraged to do so by an Oregonian, my mentor in most things horticultural. He offered no explanation, so I have none to give you. All I know is, hugging that tree felt awfully good.

A. menziesii is easily identified by its sleek, papery, burnt-orange bark peeling to a lascivious smoothness too stimulating to be legal. Clusters of white, heather-bell blossoms give way to a profusion of tiny orange-red fruits. It's native from Northern California to British Columbia and inhabits a variety of sites, from hot, dry lowlands to windswept ridgetops 5,000 feet high. Madrone grows on rock at the northern end of its range, but farther south where the rainfall is less ample, it grows in grasslands and forests.

Stunningly adaptable in the wild, *A. menziesii* is less than flawless in the home garden. Given its preference for the harsh life (hot sun, exposed bluffs, and summerlong drought), the plant is less resilient in a pampered garden setting here in the Pacific Northwest. If overwatered or nicked by a lawn mower, it can fall prey to a gross assortment of fungal diseases, including root rot, which can be fatal in a poorly drained site.

I tell you all this not to dissuade you, but to alert you. Losing a cherished madrone has got to hurt. Another option is to try your hand at the Mediterranean hybrid, *A.* 'Marina', all in all a better garden plant. It has similarly gorgeous bark, pink-blushed fall flowers, and slightly larger, shockingly bright fruit. It's also less fussy, and more resistant to disease, though reportedly less handy.

But if you've got the room, the patience, and access to seed or seedlings (digging them out of the wild is *not* an option), plant a grove of *A. menziesii* and then practice what the dean of Northwest native plant gurus, Arthur Kruckeberg, calls, "studied neglect." Choose the right site—the edge of a woodland, away from lawn mowers and overhead sprinklers. Water carefully until established, then leave them be. Otherwise, should you opt to simply admire them in the wild, be sure to give a big guy a hug for me.

A. menziesii

Azara

Working with broadleaf evergreens in the garden is a lot like adding flour to cookie dough. Too little and you're eating shapeless glop (a sodden winter border); too much, and the density will make you choke. But at least flour is inherently light-textured. Not so broadleaf evergreens, which often weigh a psychological ton, as proved by such paragons of grace as camellia, laurel, viburnum, rhodie, and aucuba.

A. serrata

Yet wasting away in undeserved anonymity is a textural lightweight named *Azara*, with all the suppleness of an interpretive dancer and the polish of a Pam-sprayed pan.

Azaras are native to Chile and Argentina, where they grow at the edge of woodlands and near lakes. They like life well-drained and wouldn't say no to supplemental summer water (though mine was never asked, and it pulled through). At least six species are garden gems of varying hardiness, but after an unusual 15°F winter, the winners are *A. serrata* and *A. microphylla*, the latter known as boxleaf azara.

What a sweetheart of a small tree, this *A. microphylla*, with its lithe sprays of glossy, crowded half-inch leaves. Like most azaras, it has a habit that is irregular, airy, and sculptural, described to perfection by Graham Stuart Thomas as "fern frond branches." Its foliage sparkles in part-shade (better morning than afternoon sun), but it doesn't take up much visual space; even at fifteen feet (maximum, twenty feet) tall, it seems little more than a mobile for a breeze to pass through.

Then comes late February, and with it the smell of spring. *A. microphylla*'s tiny, abundant greenish-yellow flowers are deliciously scented with what some describe as vanilla and others as white chocolate. Either way, you can't lose—except, I fear, in severe winters, when

the facts

BOTANICAL NAME:
Azara

SOUNDS LIKE:
A czar a

COMMON NAME:
Azara

TYPE:
Delicately textured, small evergreen tree, 12 to 20 feet

BASIC NEEDS:
Light shade to sun (preferably morning), well drained soil

WORST ENEMY:
Cold and wind (cold hardiness varies among species; choose wisely)

BEST ADVICE:
Admire someone else's if your winter lows hover in the single digits

stems can die back and flower buds will burn. Not to worry, though; the tree itself will be fine.

Though visitors to my garden are generally few and far between (I'm a fair-weather host in the best of times), those who see my *A. serrata* in winter are instantly smitten with its foliage. In late spring, they're swooning from its sweet fragrance as tons of golden-yellow, multistamened flower clusters cozy along its stalks.

But even without ornamentation, the plant is a wonder because of the shape and arrangement of its two very different kinds of leaves (a characteristic shared by several azaras). First there's the true leaf, a two-inch-long oblong, finely toothed around the edges. Then there's the stipule, a leaflike afterthought at the base of each leaf and in pairs along the stem. These scampering stipules, the size of thumbnails, have got to be the most endearing little circles of greenery you'll ever see, running along the branches like the shiny padded keys on a flute.

The juxtaposition of the two leaf forms — lean and mature versus chubby and mischievous — really gets me, but I'll understand if you're not so easily moved. Consider, then, how this azara braved a 15°F winter: not one marred leaf. I'm less optimistic about getting flowers, but I think the problem may be spite, since I withheld water last summer. When (oh when!) it gets hot again, my *A. serrata* will not want.

gimme more

All right, but give 'em shelter if your weather is consistently colder than 10°F:

A. dentata:
Much like *A. serrata*, with smaller leaves that have downy undersides; late-spring flowers; needs protection; to 12 feet

A. integrifolia:
Foliage almost entirely without toothed edges; to 12 feet

A. integrifolia 'Variegata':
Stunning selection with pink, green, and yellow leaves

A. lanceolata:
Particularly elegant form, though the least hardy; spring flowers; to 20 feet

A. microphylla 'Variegata':
Gorgeous form of boxleaf with leaves edged in creamy white; extremely dainty and slow growing; more tender and needing protection from full sun; to 15 feet

Azara

Chimonanthus praecox

DECIDUOUS SHRUB

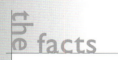

the facts

BOTANICAL NAME:
Chimonanthus praecox

SOUNDS LIKE:
Why does man
fuss knee socks

COMMON NAME:
Wintersweet

TYPE:
Multistemmed deciduous
shrub, fountainlike to leggy;
10 to 15 feet

BASIC NEEDS:
Full sun to morning
shade, ordinary soil,
decent drainage

WORST ENEMY:
Bad pruning makes it ugly;
take out old canes
after flowering

BEST ADVICE:
Not for the small garden
but delightful by path,
porch, or corner; protect in
single-digit weather

I was walking down a barren street in suburban Maryland one day when a sweet smell hit me right between the eyes. I stopped short and started sniffing—a trick I learned from my beagle, Della—but found nothing of consequence nearby. I looked up into the trees for a flowering vine, looked under shrubs for a handful of bulbs, and searched the block for a feminine form. Thinking it was heartbreak playing tricks on me, I sniffed my scarf for traces of a bygone guy.

Finally, I found the source, and boy was it ugly (would that he had been, too). "It" was a miserably pruned mass of ragged, leafless branches that could have been quince or forsythia, except that it was way too soon for either of those shrubs to be in bloom. Its thimble-sized flowers, inconspicuously huddled along the branches, were a pale yellow with an inner purple stain.

With precious little else going on in the landscape, the sensual impact of this plant was all-consuming. It was as if I'd walked into a commercial for one of those floral emission devices that turn a bathroom into a meadow or a deer-infested forest glade. The day seemed to virtually brighten up around me; the scent put a skip in my step. Kissed by the sweet breath of spring, the beagle and I danced all the way home.

At least that's how I remember it.

Such is the power of *Chimonanthus praecox,* known familiarly as wintersweet. It ranks right up there with lilacs and magnolias for superb flower fragrance, along with the similarly uncelebrated winter honeysuckle, *Lonicera standishii.* Its scent is neither cloying nor overpowering, but lemonlike and spicy; a branch or two does wonders in a living room vase.

C. praecox

The blossoms of the unimproved species are waxy and translucent and, as I've said, not very showy, but two selections, 'Luteus' (possibly the same as 'Concolor') and 'Grandiflorus', have dramatically deeper yellow blooms. However, I'm not quite convinced the selections are worth the extra cost, since the point is the plant's fragrance, which, unfortunately, is pretty much the sum of its charms.

After leafing out in spring, *C. praecox* turns back into a pumpkin, with coarse almond-shaped leaves on an upright, leggy, twelve- to fifteen-foot mound that adds bulk but little else to the landscape. It's by no means an eyesore; it simply becomes irrelevant, which is not necessarily bad (think lilac). Underplant it with spring bulbs, drape it in summer-blooming vines, mix it with autumn-lit shrubs, and you'll forget it's even there.

Until one dreary winter day when both you and the landscape are feeling a bit bereft, and a ray of sun ignites a wintersweet blossom. Suddenly, the air is redolent of romance and possibility, despite the fact that you can't remember what she looked like or have all but forgotten his name.

Chimonanthus praecox

Choisya

Choisya ternata is to the English what Japanese holly is to many of us: inert and institutional. "It's a plant that's apt to meet, unfairly, with opprobrium," writes Jane Taylor in *The Milder Garden*, "from people who associate it with seaside boarding houses, or perhaps with boarding school."

Opprobrium! Talk about getting your knickers in a twist, though it's no surprise how powerful plant associations can be. Luckily, growing *C. ternata* is not yet cause for derision in the Northwest. It's a robust border shrub that sparkles in full sun like a chubby kid with a scrubbed face.

Commonly known as Mexican orange, it has a dense, domed habit, leaves that are aromatic when crushed, and a tendency to become smothered in fragrant white flower clusters beginning in early spring. It's resistant to diseases and pests and, unless it's knocked back to the ground by a really nasty winter, its shiny, vinyl leaves are evergreen.

I could see, though, how its very utilitarianism works against the Mexican orange, a fate familiar to many a broadleaf plant. Look what happened to *Photinia*, a.k.a. red tip (pronounced ray-yud tip), a shrub that plantsman Michael Dirr describes as "so overused that the term nauseous is not sufficiently applicable."

If you're not in the market for generic greenery, the Mexican orange also comes in lemon-lime. *C. ternata* 'Sundance' was introduced in 1986; it has incredibly striking foliage that emerges brilliant yellow and fades only gently. It is smaller than the straight species, growing to about five feet, and its early-spring flowers have the same heady, orange-blossom scent. Word is it's not nearly as floriferous, but you grow this one for the winter glow. Siting is trickier with this variety: In full sun it looks chlorotic, and in too much shade it's just green. Ideally, it should bask in the morning sun and nap through the hottest part of the afternoon to reach its screaming chartreuse prime.

the facts

BOTANICAL NAME:
Choisya

SOUNDS LIKE:
Boise yuh

COMMON NAME:
Mexican orange

TYPE:
Compact, rounded evergreen shrub, 3 to 8 feet

BASIC NEEDS:
Full to part sun; even moisture; well-drained soil

WORST ENEMY:
Prolonged single-digit winters

BEST ADVICE:
It may die back to ground in a bad winter (read: 0°F), but will come right back

C. ternata 'Sundance'

Lastly, there's a choisya hybrid (*C. arizonica* × *C. ternata*) that I hesitate to write about because it's fated to become overexposed, it's just so good. 'Aztec Pearl' was introduced by the English nursery Hillier's in 1990, fast became a darling of English public-planting schemes, and is now showing up on these shores. Its long-fingered, deeply divided, lustrous leaflets are strongly reminiscent of the deliciously shapely digits of *Helleborus foetidus*, resulting in one impressive, amazingly airy shrub.

It looks unlikely that 'Aztec Pearl' is either as heavy or as sweet a bloomer as *C. ternata*—the flowers on mine were just adequate, and the fragrance was negligible—but there's no question that with this introduction, Hillier's has gone a long way to vindicate the genus.

Choisya

175

Clematis cirrhosa

EVERGREEN VINE

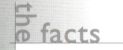

the facts

BOTANICAL NAME:
Clematis cirrhosa

SOUNDS LIKE:
Feminist mimosa

COMMON NAME:
Clematis

TYPE:
Vigorous, finely textured
evergreen vine, to 20 feet

BASIC NEEDS:
Sun to part shade;
good drainage

WORST ENEMY:
Overdoing it on the shade

BEST ADVICE:
Plant on a sheltered south
or southwest facing wall;
use annual vines for
summer color

The printed word regarding the winter-blooming clematis, *Clematis cirrhosa,* is such a mass of contradictions that it's hard to tell whether the plant's a sissy or a brute.

In the margins of my slide list from a talk given in Portland, Oregon, by Malcolm Oviatt-Ham, then president of the International Clematis Society, I quote him as calling *C. cirrhosa* var. *balaerica* (syn. *C. balaerica*) a thug, an aggressive grower that reaches thirty feet in the wild. But almost every other line written about this plant and its brethren says they are tender and need shelter from cold and wind (one Oregon grower even writes, "a nearly frost-free location is required").

So I look to my own *C. cirrhosa* a month after a sustained December freeze and what do I see (other than a miserably grown specimen that survived months in a four-inch pot before getting planted in a dark, unwatered corner)?

One tough little guy.

C. cirrhosa is native to the Mediterranean and would be happier than a paparazzo at Cannes in a hot, sunny location with good drainage. Yet Northwest-grown specimens prove that the plant's not only adaptable, but sometimes unstoppable (for instance, on a west-facing wall). Given that it's evergreen and shows its head when few other plants dare, this can be a very good thing.

Though virtually unknown compared with its glossy, laurel-leaved rival *C. armandii*—which, admittedly, is a whole lot showier—*C. cirrhosa* offers a much more dissected, delicate texture, and foliage that does not get nearly as battered and blackened when the weather gets rough.

Its November to February flowers are more delicate, too: pendulous, half-open bells of a papery texture, roughly two inches across, with a pure soft-yellow color (*C. cirrhosa* var. *balaerica* is similar, with smatterings of reddish speckles inside the bells). Their citrus

C. cirrhosa 'Freckles

fragrance has far more impact in a room than out in the cold. "I picked a trail [a trailing stem of the vine] from the garden yester-day afternoon," writes plantsman Christopher Lloyd, "boiled its stems for forty seconds, immersed it in water for an hour and it stands radiantly before me. [The flowers] look like mottled eggs." Yes, you can try this at home. *C. cirrhosa* var. *balaerica*'s mottling clearly enamored English clematis grower Raymond Evi-son — author of *The Gardener's Guide to Growing Clematis* — who, in the late 1980s, introduced a cultivar called 'Freckles'. Its four-petaled (actually, four-tepaled) flowers are larger than those of the species — up to three inches — and its base color a more creamy pink, with mottling that's way past just freckling; more like pointillism en route to blotch.

'Freckles' is not yet abundant in the trade here in the United States compared to you-know-where. Those Brits are already anticipating son of 'Freckles', a New Zealand introduction called 'Landsdowne Gem'. These days, when it comes to clematis, the bell tolls from down under — silvery gray flower bells painted solid maroon inside.

Cornus

DECIDUOUS SHRUB

the facts

BOTANICAL NAME:
Cornus

SOUNDS LIKE:
Warn us

COMMON NAME:
Shrubby dogwood

TYPE:
Upright, multistemmed,
twiggy spreading shrub,
4 to 8 feet

BASIC NEEDS:
Average to wet soil; twig
color is better in full sun

WORST ENEMY:
Drought

BEST ADVICE:
For best stem color, once
plants are 3 years old, cut
stems back to ground
every spring

Luscious mahogany. Riotous coral. Shimmering lemon-lime. 'Tis the season, all right, for every conceivable multicolored wrapping. You just have to look under the right tree.

Here's a tip: Check out the various species of shrubby dogwoods, those multistemmed cousins of the well-known spring bloomer. These unlikely treasures (with a penchant for soil that's anywhere from evenly moist to sodden) spend most of the year as highly adaptable and serviceable fillers.

As digits drop, though, and days shorten, these unassuming frogs become princes of fortune, their formerly drab stems alchemized by temperature and time. Olive green becomes chartreuse-yellow, and muddy red turns jeweled pink; masses of nondescript foliage become thickets of colorful, crisscrossed pick-up sticks.

One of the most astonishing plantings of shrubby dogwood I've ever seen is at a private garden near Seattle, where the pondside reflection of several species is so kaleidoscopic the colors seem to sweeten the air. Even more surprising is how easy it is to make an impact with these utilitarian plants; all it takes is sun, absence of drought, and thoughtful placement to capitalize on their icy winter glaze.

Let's say you have an evergreen hedge backing up a perennial border, or a dark green house surrounded by mixed shrubs. No doubt both looked fine in summer, but they probably seem terminally monochromatic now. To stir things up, plant a couple of variegated *Cornus stolonifera* 'Silver and Gold', either integrating them into the existing plantings or replacing a couple of generic evergreen balls. The reward will be instantaneous—not to mention year-round—with neon yellow stems in winter and creamy white, variegated leaves the rest of the year.

Or perhaps you live in an off-white house, now bereft of colorful foliage (ah, those Japanese maples—can't you still feel their heat?).

C. stolonifera
'Silver and Gold'

If the tree at your picture window is limbed up far enough, tuck three *C. sanguinea* 'Midwinter Fire' beneath (just be sure they have plenty of sun). These beauties have electric stems that glow red, orange, and yellow—the rival of any maple—and need only be cut back to the ground in spring to ensure next winter's show.

If you're lucky enough to have a natural pond or stream on your property and wouldn't mind some fast-growing, colonizing shrubs, mass a few flavors, selected for their winter color along its banks (winter's also the best time of year to choose shrubby dogwoods). Consider a juxtaposition of bright reds and yellows, such as *C. alba* 'Cardinal' and *C. stolonifera* 'Flaviramea', then throw in a few plumes of the smoky-purple arctic willow, *Salix purpurea* 'Nana'.

The last word in shrubby dogwood is for the avant-gardeners among you (who need not be told the trend is black): *C. alba* 'Kesselringii'. More a sumptuous, moody purple than a true black (also an apt description of its emerging foliage when grown in full sun), this cultivar demands the right setting to strut its stuff, whether lit from beneath with orange *Carex*, from behind by *C. stolonifera* 'Silver and Gold', or from above with manna from heaven, its black limbs frosted in snow.

gimme more

C. alba cultivars:
'Elegantissima':
  Red-purple stems, white variegated leaves
'Gouchaltii':
  Bright red stems, yellow-and-pink variegated leaves
'Ivory Halo':
  Similar to 'Elegantissima', more compact
'Spaethii':
  Red stems, golden variegation

C. stolonifera (syn. C. sericea)
'Cardinal':
  Cherry-red stems
'Kelseyi':
  Orange-red stems, dwarf
'Sunshine':
  Red stems, golden yellow leaves

Cornus

Corylopsis

DECIDUOUS SHRUB

C. pauciflora

the facts

BOTANICAL NAME:
Corylopsis

SOUNDS LIKE:
Cora lops this

COMMON NAME:
Buttercup winter hazel
(*C. pauciflora*), spike winter
hazel (*C. spicata*)

TYPE:
Wide-spreading, dense, late-
winter-blooming deciduous
shrub; size variable

BASIC NEEDS:
Sun to part shade, good
drainage, adaptable

WORST ENEMY:
Drought

BEST ADVICE:
A must-have late-winter
confection; choose species
by best size and shape for
your garden and underplant
with gobs of well-timed
blue (*Pulmonaria, Ipheion,*
you name it)

Love forsythia but hate its messy shape? Hate forsythia but love yellow in spring? Wish I'd stop asking questions and just get on with it? Buy a winter hazel. Now. Either that or, come late winter, get thee to an arboretum and treat yourself to one of the season's great gifts, *Corylopsis pauciflora.*

This increasingly popular member of the witch hazel family drips buttercup yellow blossoms in late winter—not the starburst straps of *Hamamelis* but the pendulous chimes of *Ribes* (flowering currant), each an exquisitely carved cluster of great distinction. By comparison, the flowers of forsythia seem coarse and windblown.

The color's classy, too, more pastel than opaque, a moderating companion for louder bulbs such as brilliant dwarf daffodils or fat Dutch crocus. Quite ample on its own (the species name *pauciflora,* meaning "few-flowered," refers to the size of the clusters, not the number), the buttercup winter hazel is at its most dazzling against a dark background.

Unlike forsythia, *C. pauciflora* works all year for a living, with a handsome habit and a modest average height of five feet, which keeps it from overwhelming a small space. Its leaves are heavily veined like those of the witch hazels but are deliciously diminutive; frankly, I'm undone even by its compelling, bite-size leaf buds. Come fall, the buttercup winter hazel can have a good amber color but doesn't compare with witch hazel's autumn display.

Admittedly, I inherited my woody-plants professor's prejudice toward the refined *C. pauciflora,* but I saw some killer specimens of the spike winter hazel, *C. spicata,* at a flower show. This species has a much more open and spreading habit, capable of a ten-foot wingspan, with flower chains decorated by red-purple anthers, the cluster's length probably twice that of *C. pauci-flora*. *C. spicata* flowers happily in part shade but, unlike *C. pauciflora*, welcomes full sun.

Certainly, the spike winter hazel makes a more dramatic specimen if you have the space and crave the presence (even after the flowers, its young leaves emerge a show-stopping purple bronze). Both species are equally hardy, though once in a blue moon the flower buds may be damaged by an unexpected late freeze.

For –20°F hardiness, the species of choice is the fragrant winter hazel, *C. glabrescens* (or its cultivar 'Longwood Chimes'), capable of twelve to fifteen feet and a similar spread. The trick to using this imposing form—and *C. spicata*, for that matter—is to limb it up into a multistemmed tree and make it a scaffold for summer blooming vines.

If you're feeling overwhelmed with choices, let space be the deciding factor and promptly turn the page. Otherwise, you're likely to find out about *C.* 'Winterthur', reputedly a cross between *C. spicata* and *C. pauciflora*, introduced at the du Pont estate garden of that name in Delaware. It's said to combine the fragrance of one parent with the fine, dense habit of the other; after twenty-five years, the original specimen remains twelve feet tall. All of which takes me full circle as I repeat: If you can find it, buy it.

There's lots of confusion in the trade about species names.

C. coreana:
Heart-shaped foliage to 4 inches; from South Korea

C. platypetala (syn. C. sinensis var. calvescens):
Particularly beautiful flowers; one of the largest, to 15 feet

C. sinensis var. sinensis (syn. C. willmottiae):
Citrus-sweet, longest flower clusters to 5 inches; bronze new growth

'Spring Purple':
Cultivar with reddish-purple new growth

Cryptomeria japonica 'Spiralis'

CONIFER

My father's mother had wavy hair that fit like a helmet. My mother's mother wore hers in a soft Gibson girl pile. Consequently, the nostalgic plant name 'Granny's ringlets' doesn't strike a familiar chord, though it does conjure up a rather dissonant picture of both my grandmas in dreadlocks. Oy!

I suspect that is not the image that inspired the common name for *Cryptomeria japonica* 'Spiralis', a richly textured Japanese cedar with curly rings reminiscent of what (someone's) granny used to wear. The effect is created by spirally curved, inward-pointing needles that twist covetously around the plant's flexible stems—cascading locks on a seemingly restless tree.

In fact, *C. japonica* 'Spiralis' is the very paradigm of stability, with a body so dense and spongy you could confidently fall into its arms. The plant encourages that kind of interaction because it's just so tactile, its gold-braided limbs and twisted fringes begging to be touched.

At maturity, 'Spiralis' is a formal, conical evergreen, but in its early years it's somewhat wayward. The reason is this: New plants are grown from side-branch cuttings, so their inclination is to grow sideways. "They need to learn apical dominance," says Oregon conifer wizard Don Howse. It takes a good four years for the plant to develop a central, upright stem (known as the leader), which will eventually become the tree's trunk.

Those early years, however comical, are likely to be misunderstood. Howse often sees young 'Spiralis' mislabeled and sold as a prostrate shrub rather than as a cone-shaped tree. His own once-gawky specimen is now twenty feet tall and eight feet wide, a proper and masterful landscape presence, flawlessly branched from head to toe.

Now for colors: 'Spiralis' comes in two. With afternoon shade, it develops soft lime spring-like growth, while in full sun it tends toward yellow-gold and can even look a bit burned (contrary to appearance, though, this plant will not sun-scald). Its color is uniform

C. japonica 'Spiralis'

throughout, but the twisted leaves give the impression of being two-tone; until this writing, I'd remembered it as variegated, such was the image in my (fantasy-prone) mind's eye.

If you've got some big bored rhodies in all-morning sun, plant a lime-green 'Spiralis' among them to wake things up. If you don't have the room but still want the ringlets, consider *C. japonica* 'Spiraliter Falcata', a probable sport of the spiral-leaved giant. Maxing out at five feet by five feet (it's a slow grower), it's been called the 'Harry Lauder' of cryptomerias (a reference to the contorted filbert), with stems and branches that twist and curl. It's good for a light touch of whimsy in a not-quite-mixed-enough border.

Daphne

DECIDUOUS OR EVERGREEN SHRUB

the facts

the facts

BOTANICAL NAME:
Daphne

SOUNDS LIKE:
Calf knee

COMMON NAME:
February daphne (D. mezereum), winter daphne (D. odora)

TYPE:
Small, twiggy, rounded to upright late-winter-blooming shrubs, to 4 feet

BASIC NEEDS:
Sun to some shade; good drainage; a cool root run

WORST ENEMY:
Sustained cold in low teens for D. odora; also, most daphnes resent having their rootballs disturbed

BEST ADVICE:
Evergreen species including D. odora are unpredictable; one day you think they're thriving, and the next day they're dead—it's not your fault; handle balled-and-burlapped shrubs carefully when planting

I logged into cyberspace the other day to learn more about the February-blooming daphne, *D. mezereum,* and ended up downloading a list of ways I might put an end to my life.

In addition to "Asphyxiation," "Bullet," and "Slitting Wrist or Other," the categories included "Poisonous Plants." I read that although the berries of *D. mezereum* taste horrid, it takes only a dozen or so to cause death.

So the first thing I want to say about this fabulous late-winter bloomer is that if you have kids, don't plant it. The color and sparkle of its red fruits are too alluring, and it's not worth the risk.

(Pets, however, rarely if ever become fatally ill from ingesting outdoor plants, according to my local emergency-clinic veterinarian. She treats far more dogs for eating bone meal or rotting compost than berries or leaves.)

If you have no kids, you need have no worries about the February daphne, and you have an abundance of reasons to grow it: Fragrant, rosy-purple flowers on dramatically upright, naked stems; bright and tidy blue-green leaves; extreme hardiness; and, for a daphne, it's relatively trouble free. It blossoms before most things have leafed out and berries while most things are in flower—always a standout, ahead of the crowd.

A couple of varieties are knocking around with deeper-hued flowers or late-fall blooms, but the most touted and readily available form is the white-flowered 'Alba', with abundant amber-yellow summer fruit. It's great in flower and the berries are unusual, if not as startling as the similarly poisoned-apple-red ones.

I imagine most of you have inhaled deeply in the presence of the evergreen winter daphne, *D. odora*—or more possibly, its variegated selection 'Aureo-marginata'—and have since sworn never to be without one. Enough said. For those who suspect me of gross exaggeration, I urge you to visit one, at a friend's garden or a public garden, and find out why this is a must-have plant. The winter daphne sets a standard for flower fragrance that is well beyond most genera, a rich orange-blossom scent that manages to be sophisticated and giddy in one fell swoon.

As luck would have it, *D. odora* is also eager to be in bloom. An extremely young shrub in my last garden displayed sporadic pinky purple stars for a good eight months. A few steps away, the indispensable 'Aureo-marginata' vied for more than equal time, its evergreen leaves stenciled with creamy yellow margins on a chubby shrub that is hardier than the straight species. Unfortunately (I feel like I'm doing a lot of giving and taking away here), "hardier" only takes us to 15°F or so. So if you're toddler free, grow the February daphne for a new lease on life.

D. mezereum

Dichroa febrifuga

BROADLEAF EVERGREEN

BOTANICAL NAME:
Dichroa febrifuga

SOUNDS LIKE:
Might grow allegro
fugue ah

COMMON NAME:
Dichroa

TYPE:
Small, mounded evergreen,
to 2 feet (6 feet in the wild)

BASIC NEEDS:
Light shade, good
drainage; avoid prolonged
single-digit exposure

WORST ENEMY:
Exacting expectations
about the berry's desired
shade of blue

BEST ADVICE:
Needs a temperate, pam-
pered spot unless you're
sure its origins were hardy

"Why make so much of fragmentary blue . . .When heaven presents in sheets the solid hue?" Robert Frost asks in his poem, "Fragmentary Blue."

Exactly my question. What's the big deal in a little bit of blue? Particularly in a plant? Yet whenever I encounter a blue flower, bean, or berry, the effect is inexplicable wonder.

Part of the reason may be that it's a color rich with emotional complexity: innocence (baby blue eyes), intensity (deep blue sea), optimism (blue skies), despair (the blues). In a flower, it tends to seem distant and somewhat surreal. Time and again, whether it's the pastel wash of 'Blue Wave' hydrangeas or the seemingly artificial intensity of *Lithodora* 'Grace Ward', someone is bound to react by saying, "It can't be real!"

Though it's not one of my preferred colors in socks, sheets, or sofas, I am a sucker for blue in plants—and I was, indeed, sucker-punched one winter day, walking through a friend's woodland garden. The place is like a big Easter egg hunt anyway, so I wasn't unaccustomed to being surprised, but when he showed me the blue fruit on his own seed-collected specimen of *Dichroa febrifuga,* I figured he was having me on.

The sight was positively, achingly beautiful, and seemingly staged—these small pools of lapis lazuli tears set off by lustrous, rich evergreen leaves. The plant itself was no more than an intimate dwarf mound, but its impact was enormous, with all the contradictions of sweetness and sadness inherent in the color blue.

In fruit, dichroa seems pretty exotic, but it's bound to look familiar in its soft blue bloom. Like a lacecap hydrangea, perhaps? No coincidence; they're close relatives. Admittedly, it doesn't have quite the flower power of hydrangea, nor its generous, billowing mass, but dichroa also functions quite differently in the landscape. It's a small gem, easily integrated into a woodland, always capable of surprise though never presuming to claim center stage.

Best not to be too presumptuous about it, either, since this is an extremely changeable species, with immense variation in berry color (sapphire blue to pansy purple), leaf shape, and— heads up!—hardiness. It's a good idea to ask the nursery you buy it from what kind of winters the parent plant's been through. In any event, it can't hurt to give the plant a cushy, protected spot.

Now here's a bonus: In the unlikely event that you cross paths with malaria, know that the root of dichroa is a centuries-old cure. Its use is fundamental to Chinese herbalism, where its considerable— and slightly toxic—powers are harnessed for human good.

D. febrifuga

Edgeworthia

DECIDUOUS SHRUB

Wintertime, and the living's not easy. Plants are frozen, and the tempers are high. Hebe's toast, and the rosemary's cringing. If this is called temperate, why do I want to cry?

Let's take the long view. Yesterday, the air was redolent of winter honeysuckle *(Lonicera standishii)* and wintersweet *(Chimonanthus praecox)*. Today, those same flowers are encased in ice. But tomorrow, a sun break will awaken the dormant buds of *Edgeworthia*, and nature will toss us a few more fragrant crumbs.

Edgeworthia's common name, paper bush, comes from its utilitarian bark, which is processed into a high-grade paper product in Japan and China. It was also planted in abundance as a resource crop in southern China, where it's evidently still common in hedgerows. The bark is flaky and cinnamon-colored in youth, and the branches are incredibly bendable, which explains its other name, knot plant.

Known to appear as early as January, though more typically in February, the flowers of the paper bush emerge from silky-white button buds that begin to fatten up in fall. Like those of its close kin *Daphne*, its blossoms are clustered; they nod like bite-size sunflowers off the end of the plant's stout stems. Lemon yellow upon opening, they soften to a creamy custard, which some say also describes their fragrance: warm, rich, lightly sweet, and particularly soothing at this often trying time of year.

The plant's native habitat is the woodland edge, often streamside, which tells you something about its culture. We're not talking drought resistance; on the contrary, edgeworthia needs evenly moist soil through summer. Because it grows vigorously from the base, it quickly makes a multistemmed shrub, but it's far more elegant trained into a domed, single-trunked three- to five-foot tree.

While researching edgeworthia, I stumbled into a small botanical hornet's nest. Are the species *E. papyrifera* and *E. chrysantha* in fact one and the same? (You're kidding; you haven't been able to sleep, either?) Well, despite dissension in the ranks, it looks entirely likely. A true second species, however, *E. gardneri*, is said to be distinguished from the identical twins by bolder foliage, some leaves being five to seven inches long. Incidentally, a completely misnamed cultivar of paper bush should be showing up in the near future. *E. chrysantha* 'Rubra' is not remotely red. Instead, it's a deliciously bright orange that hits just the right temperature if you like your winter colors warm as (versus burnt as) toast.

E. chrysantha

Garrya

BROADLEAF EVERGREEN

BOTANICAL NAME:
Garrya

SOUNDS LIKE:
Nary a

COMMON NAME:
Silk-tassel bush

TYPE:
Coarse, rounded to spreading evergreen, 6 to 10 feet

BASIC NEEDS:
Sun to part shade, well-drained soil

WORST ENEMY:
Exposed sites with cold whipping winds, which can cause leaf burn

BEST ADVICE:
For proven 10°F hardiness, get Garrya x issaquahensis (great espaliered up against a wall); also benefits from an evergreen background

Forgive me, but I must get this out of my system.

Garrya, Indiana, Garrya Indiana, not Louisiana, Paris, France, New York or Rome . . .

But GARRya, Indiana, Garrya INdiana, Garrya, IndiANA, My Home Sweet Home!

Thanks. I needed that.

Seen in its glory, Northwest native silk-tassel bush makes me want to break out in song. It's one of those powerful and extremely trendy plants that can both hold its own as a showy ornamental and suggest a strong sense of place (in this case, Portland, not Gary). Certainly we've no shortage of native treasures, whether madrone, *Mahonia*, or salal, but our *Garrya* species are more versatile than the peeling-barked tree and more charismatic than the broadleaf evergreen shrubs, combining texture, elegance, and evergreen foliage on startlingly different and easy-to-grow plants.

It's actually pretty astonishing that *Garrya elliptica* isn't more of a Northwest signature shrub, since its irregular shape is still basically conservative and its maintenance is pretty low. The plant's got ample everyday attributes, including strikingly different gray-washed foliage, with woolly undersides revealed by dramatically undulating leaves. It really doesn't have a bad season, only a less showy one, much like camellias and rhodies do.

But all that's after the fact. The primary reason to grow garrya is to extend the holiday season an extra two months, since the silk tassel bush decked out in its winter finery is easily as joyous as a tinseled tree. Weather depending, the shrub can flower within days of the New Year and outlast all but the most heartfelt resolutions.

Garrya's long, flowering strands resemble tiny teacups stacked upside down, a thumbnail wide and sometimes more than a foot long. These pale catkins hang from the tip of every shoot and sway like strings of beads in a breeze. The effect is dazzling but not ostentatious

G. elliptica 'James Roof'

because the teacups' colors are subdued—oyster gray with a frill of yellow stamens, for an overall appearance of creamy, celery green.

Flower and foliage color vary depending on species and variety, of which there are several. If your priority is flower length, nothing can touch, the *G. elliptica* cultivars 'Evie' and 'James Roof,' with nearly foot-long catkins. For dark green foliage—as well as exceptional hardiness—you'll want the silk-tassel hybrid *G.* × *issaquahensis* (*G. elliptica* × *G. fremontii*), or its showy selection 'Pat Ballard'.

A word before bringing your garrya home: Make sure it's a guy (or that you've bought one of each). The female has nice fruits but pales in plumage. Named cultivars are dependable, but if you're after the straight species, it's hard to know (tell me about it). Your best bet is to shop in winter, while the plants are still in bloom.

Grevillea victoriae

BROADLEAF EVERGREEN

A friend of mine does not embrace the concept of winter interest in the garden. He prefers to rest his, uh, senses (personally, I suspect he simply can't be bothered learning the names of new plants). So in introducing *Grevillea victoriae* I have two objectives: To test the strength of his convictions, and to redefine the winter-interest cliché.

I saw my first plant last January at the University of British Columbia Botanical Garden in Vancouver, B.C. This sprawling, silvery leaved, imposing specimen really threw me off, since I'd never encountered such color and bravado in a winter-blooming plant. From a distance, I thought all the excitement was its new growth (reminiscent of the emerging foliage on *Pieris*), so when I realized the shrub was actually in flower, you can imagine my shrieks of surprise.

Close-up, the head-high, yards-wide plant was bursting at the tips with orange-red, honeysuckle-like clusters, the ends of each strapping petal dramatically curled under like talons. The blossoms,

G. victoriae

each about an inch across, hung in racemes off the branch ends.

What made the plant particularly striking was the contrast between flowers and leaves: The endless billows of gray-green foliage seemed to toss the hot-colored blossoms off the shrub. We're talking midwinter bonfire here, or an out-of-season burning bush, particularly when you consider *G. victoriae*'s potential size (ten feet by ten feet).

But wait: It gets better. Mike Lee of Colvos Creek Nursery outside Seattle—who, in the early 1980s, was one of the first nurserymen to bring *G. victoriae* to the Northwest—says his own plants have been known to throw off the odd flower as ludicrously late as May. He also points out that the shrub typically forms its metallic, coppery buds by late summer. All of this adds up to a bud-to-bloom-to-bust sequence that could last two-thirds of the year.

Want to talk hardiness? Love to. Tigard, Oregon, plantsman Russ Archer has had his *G. victoriae* for more than ten years. That means it's survived some pretty cold winters with nothing worse than leaf burn. Mike Lee seconds that, and puts in a pitch for its frost-resistant flowers, which have remained unmolested at 20°F.

Both admit to having seriously underestimated the girth of this fast-growing shrub (Lee says from a gallon pot to six feet by six feet in three years!), and recommend putting it someplace where you can just let it go. All the better to divert Anna's hummingbirds, who just might belly up to this open bar, and to send a jolt through an otherwise sedate and sodden landscape—not to mention your winter-wary friends.

Who wouldn't want more of these disease- and drought-resistant Aussies?

G. victoriae:
'Murray Valley Queen':
Very floriferous, with coppery undersides to new leaves
'Porrinda Constance':
G. victoriae-like flowers, narrow, thin leaves

G. juniperina f. sulphurea:
Yellow flowers, bright green needle-like leaves

G. rosmarinifolia:
Crimson flowers, rosemary-gray green

Grevillea victoriae

Helleborus

H. orientalis

"Perhaps this is the place to issue a warning," writes Elizabeth Strangman in *The Gardener's Guide to Growing Hellebores.* "Hellebores are addictive, and once intrigued and ensnared by their charms it is hard to break the spell."

I'll say. Coast to coast, American gardeners are gonzo for hellebores, and don't the nurseryfolk know it. The plant's a regular pinup girl—gracing the covers of who knows how many plant catalogs this year—her open-wide, color-saturated sepals whispering sweet nothings as her provocative private parts draw you in. Even Strangman's book reads like a *Sports Illustrated* swimsuit issue, page after page of glossy close-ups with each flower at its absolute peak. Midnight purples and high-noon yellows bear witness to the sorcery of hybridization: these beauties did not emerge whole from their shells.

Most are crosses of the lenten rose, *Helleborus orientalis*, plants now available in a mind-numbing range of flower color. Some are named forms, but others are simply grouped by color, such as blueblacks, smoky purples, or pinks. I wish I could make it easy on you and select one or two cultivars, but the breeding and selection frenzy is moving too fast to keep tabs on. Your best bet is to simply buy the hybrids in flower, and let your rising pulse rate be your guide.

If I might, however, divert your attention from all this transient beauty, there are two other forms of hellebore that make superb, year-round garden plants.

We don't hear much about plants native to England, but here's one: *Helleborus foetidus*, the "stinking hellebore," named for the olfactory sensation that results from crushing its leaves. The smell's really not that bad, just slightly skunky (Strangman describes the flower's scent as "rather catty"). The blossoms are pale green and really jump out of the shade, further enhanced by their startling contrast against the hellebore's rich, olive green leaves. For my money, the foliage is worth the price of admission, each leaf divided into long elegant leaflets in that classic, palmately compound shape of cannabis leaves.

H. foetidus is adaptable to sun or shade, though happiest in humusy soil. It's not particularly long-lived, but generally leaves behind a brood of easily raised seedlings. 'Wester Flisk' is a gorgeous selection with red-tinted stems and leaf petioles and, sometimes, a red blush to its flowers.

H. × sternii
'Blackthorn Strain'

No one believes me when I say *Helleborus × sternii* is happy in full sun, but given ample moisture, it's all the more gorgeous after taking in the rays. In its best form, this cross has marbled foliage that emerges almost steely blue, with pink stems and pink-flushed flowers (which are admittedly ho-hum).

The selection 'Blackthorn Strain', made at Blackthorn Nursery in England, is thought to have the best leaf color, with the bonus of crim-son stems. For that reason, if you can find it, you might grab the named form. However, I grow both *H. × sternii* and 'Blackthorn Strain' (I paid dearly for the latter), and I can't tell the two exquisite plants apart.

Kadsura japonica 'Chirifu'

EVERGREEN VINE

The brightly variegated evergreen vine *Kadsura japonica* 'Chirifu' is currently one of the most treasured plants in my garden (soon to be rivaled by my white-budded *Ribes sanguineum*, just itching to pop). The vine is all that stands between my leafless lilac and its recurring nightmare ("I dreamt I was naked and everyone was laughing at me!"). In time, the *Kadsura* will swaddle the lilac and banish its thoughts of shame.

Kadsura japonica—the name is one letter and a light year away from the lovely tree called katsura—is an Asian native and one of only two genera in the family *Schisandraceae*. Sometimes called the magnolia vine, it comes in a couple of flavors, including plain (straight green) and variegated (either speckled or edged in vanilla). Its small spring flowers are lightly fragrant, cup-shaped, and creamy white. Evidently its fall berries are particularly ornamental—pendulous clusters of scarlet—but I wouldn't know, since I've only one plant, and it takes both a male and female for the vine to set fruit.

No doubt fruit would be an extra bonus, but if you've got the cultivar 'Chirifu', wanting more seems downright piggy. In the dead of winter, the foliage on this National Arboretum introduction reads creamy white from a distance; you've got to be close up to see the green speckling within. During the growing season, it then takes on complex variegation, none of its four-inch leaves alike, for a glossy, luminous effect

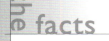

the facts

BOTANICAL NAME:
Kadsura japonica

SOUNDS LIKE:
Mad soarer

COMMON NAME:
Kadsura vine

TYPE:
Nicely behaved evergreen vine, 15 feet

BASIC NEEDS:
Part shade, well-drained soil

WORST ENEMY:
Negligent watering (file under: do as I say, not as I do)

BEST ADVICE:
Though you can grow this with more confidence in the Southeast than in the Northwest, it's worth a shot with shelter from wind and cold

that can enliven a shady corner or offer a vertical stroke of brilliance to a mixed and lightly variegated bed.

The difference between 'Chirifu' and 'Variegata' (which from its descriptions sounds very similar to the cultivar 'Fukurin') is that 'Chirifu' is shot through with variegation, while the others have irregular, creamy borders. Frankly, I doubt there's a dud in the bunch.

Less certain is hardiness, guaranteed to 10°F, but very possibly to zero in scrumptious, well-drained soil and a sheltered spot. The variegated forms prefer part shade, in which they'd no doubt be more vigorous than mine, but the 'Chirifu' I grow gets no direct sun whatsoever—at least not until it makes it past my lilac's naked knees.

K. japonica 'Chirifu'

Ophiopogon planiscapus 'Nigrescens'

EVERGREEN ORNAMENTAL GRASS

the facts

BOTANICAL NAME:
Ophiopogon planiscapus
'Nigrescens'

SOUNDS LIKE:
Sophie owe Logan, Dan
escape us, wry lessons

COMMON NAME:
Black mondo grass

TYPE:
Evergreen ornamental
grass, 6 inches

BASIC NEEDS:
Sun to part shade,
lusher with moisture but
incredibly versatile

WORST ENEMY:
No real enemy, just faster
spreading when mulched
and given adequate water

BEST ADVICE:
Why garden without it?

Black. Who knew. It lacks hue and is as dull as can be. But whether in leaves or in flowers, it may well be the trendiest turn-of-the-millennium color.

Consider what's happening in retail. Wayside Gardens in Hodges, South Carolina, has introduced 'Hillside Black Beauty'; a three-inch pot of this dark-leaved *Cimicifuga* will run you twenty-five big ones. Brothers Herbs and Peonies in Sherwood, Oregon, is pushing 'Black Panther', a hundred-dollar tree peony with flowers the color of dried blood. Gossler Farms & Nursery in Springfield, Oregon, offers a blue-black, hand-pollinated hellebore at twenty-five dollars for a two-gallon pot. The blacklist goes on.

If you're new to hort noir, there are plenty of heartthrobs from earlier fads, including 'Black Magic' elephant ears, 'Black Game-cock' iris, 'Black Barlow' columbines, 'Bowles' Black' pansies, and the much-loved 'Queen of the Night' tulips.

But most of these named selections are pretenders to the dark throne; close, but no scepter. Any lover of black plants worth his Faustian soul would trade them all for *Ophiopogon planiscapus* 'Nigrescens', black mondo grass.

Whether named 'Ebony Night', 'Arabicus', or 'Black Dragon', this is what you've got: a clumping perennial in the lily family that spreads by underground stolons to form a slowly creeping, evergreen groundcover, unfazed by severe cold (we call that zero in the Northwest; otherwise hardy to $-10°F$).

Black mondo grass is the ultimate conversation piece because no one can believe it's really black. Fact is, some of my texts insist it's a dark, dark purple. But I'll tell you what: It's the same color as my stapler, telephone, calculator, and coffee maker; and I daresay that if there were any black licorice in the house, my mondo's quarter-inch-wide, eight-inch-long leaf would hold its own.

This versatile, spidery plant has other ornamental attributes:

dainty, bell-shaped, purplish-white summer flowers, followed by lustrous, blue-black (and slightly camouflaged) fruit. It's happy in sun to part shade, and though it likes moisture, mine has learned to cope with drought.

But the best thing about black mondo is, ironically, the way it can light up the garden, making yellows, oranges, limes, and silvers all the more audacious by providing a contrast that is positively surreal. Some classic combos include black mondo amidst yellow creeping Jenny (*Lysimachia nummularia* 'Aurea') or golden hakonechloa (*H. macra* 'Aureola'); alongside orange sedge *(Carex testacea)* and blue-leaved hebe; or amidst pewter-lined heuchera and painted ferns (*Athyrium nipponicum* 'Pictum').

O. planiscapus 'Nigrescens'

To make the most of your mondo, use a liberal mix of humus and humor. Don't worry about overdoing it; in the dark days of winter, there's simply no such thing as too much fun.

Ophiopogon planiscapus 'Nigrescens'

Pinus bungeana

CONIFER

Her nickname was Lacebark and she was a living mosaic, pieced together from alabaster, ivory, amber, and jade. You know the type, with cheeks that put the glow of the moon to shame. I'd never met anyone like her, and probably never would have, had I not glanced through the Personals in the back of *The American Tree Hugger's Magazine:*

ARBOREAL DISH SEEKS CONNOISSEUR

Graceful, slender & long-legged, mother of pearl complexion with startling short dark hair, ISO stable, sun-loving gardener who believes good things come to those who wait. Your place or mine? ☎ 878-4448

She was definitely not my type—I'm not what you'd call stable—but she seemed like a nice girl, so I gave her a call. Turns out she'd had a bad time of it: one among many in a huge family, and lost among the pines; slow to develop physically, and you know how tough on a babe that can be; always kind of comely, but not so's you'd notice, and for a long time nobody did; a late bloomer professionally—turns out she loved to act— but always got passed over for the choicer roles.

Part of the baggage, she says, of being evergreen.

I told her I had some contacts in the plant world and suggested she send me her picture. I didn't want to brag, but I knew my way around this forest, and was certain I could shake down a few trees. As sure as ten dimes will buy you a dollar, the pix proved her good as her word. Fact is, Lacebark seemed just a little too good to be true.

I needed to see her in the flesh. I finagled an invitation for tea. She lived in what seemed like a Chinese

the facts

BOTANICAL NAME:
Pinus bungeana

SOUNDS LIKE:
Pieness grungy Anna

COMMON NAME:
Lacebark pine

TYPE:
Multistemmed, statuesque, broad-spreading conifer, 30 to 40 feet

BASIC NEEDS:
Full sun; well-drained soil

WORST ENEMY:
Shade and impatience

BEST ADVICE:
Though multistemmed by nature, keeping it to a single trunk will make for a more structurally sound, ice-storm-resistant tree; figure a decade before bark peels

temple garden; turns out, it was a scaled-down repli-
ca of her ancestors' sacred home. Her relatives had
lived outside Peking for centuries before the telling
events of 1831, when a visiting Russian botanist
named Aleksandr von Bunge laid eyes on the aged,
chalk-barked family and told one too many friends.

Invitations from abroad flooded in. Who could
refuse? The family dispersed via England with the
help of a guy named Fortune (man, was *he* ever on a
roll). Lacebark's branch hit our shores in 1879. They
were the toast of the town—exotic Asian emigrés were
big news those days—but here we are, several genera-
tions later, and nobody knows her name.

Watching her lustrous dark needles, her airy grace,
and her luminescent body (molded by time into patterns
and patches that changed hues with the setting sun), I
couldn't believe she'd ever been ordinary. The dame was
positively incredible. Her beauty was easily equal to that of
the legendary, mahogany-skinned Maple—I knew her as
Paperbark—but more startling because of the package she
was wrapped in.

Evergreen.

I wanted her. Badly. And I knew I could never have her. Lacebark outclassed me by a mile. I envied the landscape that would
be transformed by her presence; just by looking at her, I could tell
she'd only get more beautiful with time.

I left her with the promise that I'd tell her story, so that she might
find what she longed for so dearly: room to breathe and time to
grow. Not much, all told. As I drove away, my heart captured, my
reason under siege, I resolved to hold tight to my promise.

Tight as bark on a tree.

Pinus bungeana

Polygala chamaebuxus

DWARF BROADLEAF EVERGREEN

the facts

Every once in a while a botanical name gets stuck in my head like a catchy tune. It all started years ago with *Tradescantia,* which hit me like the Hallelujah Chorus. In fact, that's how I memorized its name—singing it to that famous chorus from Handel's *Messiah*:

TRAD-escantia! TRAD-escantia! TradesCANtia! TradesCAN tia! TradesCA-A-AN-tia!

Of course, some plant names make their own music: *Chamaecyparis* (cammaSIParris) . . . *Diascia* (deeASSeeya) . . . *Melaleuca* (mellaLUKEah) . . . each a lyric waiting for a song. Others, such as the incredibly suggestive *Polygala,* come with their own short story.

Depending on your bent, *Polygala chamaebuxus* (poLIGala cameeBUCKsus) conjures up images of either a debauched Roman emperor or a fairy-tale princess with chubby cheeks ("One day, little Polygala bought a big box of chocolates. . . ."). One look at the plant, of course, and all thoughts of depravity vanish, since we're talking an incredibly pretty little groundhugger of a shrub with dainty, orchidlike flowers.

But the common name for the genus—milkwort—makes for a rather racy story when told by Martha Barnette, author of *A Garden of Words,* a book that celebrates the language of plants. Barnette, who lives in Kentucky, is an e-mail buddy of mine who can't resist a good etymological challenge, so I put the word "milkwort" to her, and this is what she wrote:

"Ha! Well, my OED [Oxford English Dictionary] says that milkwort was 'formerly supposed to increase the milk of nurses.' Under 'Polygala' there's a 1661 notation saying it causes 'the cattle to give abundance thereof.'

"Then there's always the fun factoid," she continues, "that the Romans . . . said that the Milky Way had spurted from Juno's breasts, and that the drops that had fallen to earth had turned into lilies. English poets of the sixteenth and seventeenth centuries used the term 'milky way' to refer to 'the region of a woman's breasts' [as in] 'Behold her heav'nly face and heaving milky way.' Hooee! Hot stuff in them thar dictionaries!"

The woman definitely has a way with language—though I doubt she'd have as much success growing *P. chamaebuxus* or its prettier sister, *P. chamaebuxus* var. *grandiflora,* both unlikely candidates for Kentucky's clay soil and summer humidity. The plants are quite at home here in the Northwest, though, asking no more than good drainage and full sun (and even that's negotiable).

Yet for truly pretty late-winter-blooming evergreens, they're surprisingly underused, and it could well be their bloom time that works against them. Even if the nurseries were chock-full of these milkworts, few gardeners would be browsing the tables to see them. They're also truly tiny—we're talking four inches high—and are typically grown in rock gardens and troughs. Yet plant these boxwoodlike bushlets in a conspicuous place where their fanciful blossoms can be seen—whether at the edge of a shrub border, beneath dwarf rhodies, or mixed with edging along the front walk—and you're likely to be asked their story. Any fun factoid will do.

P. chamaebuxus

P. chamaebuxus cultivars:

'Kamniski':
Rich purple and yellow flowers, larger and more robust form; to 10 inches

'Rhodoptera':
Purplish pink and yellow flowers; smaller leaves than species

P. calcarea 'Linnet':
Gentian-blue late spring flowers; harder to find, less easy to please; 2 inches

P. vayredae:
Smaller flowers but most vivid coloring of all; linear leaves; 4 inches

Polygala chamaebuxus

Pseudocydonia sinensis

FLOWERING TREE

It seems a bit disparaging to call a plant "pseudo" anything, as if it lacked the integrity to be more than an imitation of something else. Here in the Northwest, for instance, we don't think of our mighty Douglas fir it as a false hemlock. But its genus name, *Pseudotsuga*, means just that.

I don't mean to start a chauvinist landslide in favor of reclassifying the Doug fir. But it is odd that a dozen or more plants exist which, though different enough to be given their own exclusive genera, were not quite different enough to get their own names.

Pseudocydonia sinensis, the Chinese quince, suffers from all sorts of nomenclatural baggage. You can't really call it a false quince because its fruit are indeed quince, just not the variety cultivated for preserves (or for wine, candy, juice, or even pickles, as favored in Japan). Instead, its fruits are far more useful for playing that early-adolescent contact sport, Pass the Orange; they're big and oblong—a good shape for neck-hugging— not to mention heavy and hard.

And though *P. sinensis* flowers prettily (albeit subtly and sparsely) in pink, you can't call it a flowering quince, because that name's been taken too. Flowering quince is *Chaenomeles,* that dense, thorny, spring-blooming shrub that comes in all those incomparably rich and tarty hot colors.

But in winter, when its namesakes are downright boring, *P. sinensis* glows with exfoliating bark. This handsome creature is right up there with the best of the mottled crew, in tones as warm as *Stewartia* and in patterns suggestive of lacebark pine. Stunning visually, it's also tactually irresistible, with a fluted trunk that adds rhythm to its changing surface of warm browns, olive greens, and pearly grays. This is a small tree with a dense, rounded crown and impressive peach to red leaves in late fall when grown in full sun. Its large April flowers are the color of apple blossoms, its late-spring peeling reveals chrome-yellow skin, and its magnificent fall fruits are a light lemon yellow (only the color is light; you don't want to be under them when they fall). Though these trees are easy to grow, you'll need a good eye for pruning, since young ones are awkward and need shaping. What you'll end up with for your labors is an increasingly handsome specimen, a prince of a plant denied a worthy name.

P. sinensis

Ribes sanguineum

DECIDUOUS SHRUB

the facts

BOTANICAL NAME:
Ribes sanguineum

SOUNDS LIKE:
Pie, please, an' gimme one

COMMON NAME:
Winter currant or
red-flowering currant

TYPE:
Mid-February through early
May-blooming, upright,
twiggy deciduous shrub;
5 to 12 feet

BASIC NEEDS:
Full sun to part shade, good
drainage; drought tolerant

WORST ENEMY:
Summer water

BEST ADVICE:
If you need your confidence
as a gardener boosted,
these are ridiculously easy-
to-please plants

When I was young, whether it was true or I imagined it, I often felt that my mother didn't give much credence to my opinions or observations until they were legitimized by an outside source. Consequently, I have an inordinate fondness for plants I believe have suffered similar fates.

Consider, for instance, our Northwest native winter currant, *Ribes sanguineum,* a complete joy throughout the unspoiled region for who-knows-how-many centuries. Studded with capbursts of color at a botanically bereft time of year, *R. sanguineum* had undoubtedly been celebrated by indigenous peoples up and down the Northwest coast.

But it wasn't until the arrival of the Scots that true legitimacy was conferred on the species: "discovered" (don't you hate that?) in 1793 by Archibald Menzies during his voyage with Captain George Vancouver; introduced into British commerce in 1817 by Scotsman David Douglas; popularized throughout England and cultivated into tamer forms, such as 'King Edward VII'; finally reintroduced to the United States where it won acceptance as a titled and worthy garden plant.

Thanks, Mum.

But what's done is done, and no harm for it: *R. sanguineum* is one of the all-time superb early-spring-flowering shrubs. Easy (I mean *easy*) to grow, well-mannered but amenable to severe pruning, the red-flowering currant has fabulously showy flower clusters that are usually unhindered by leaves. Time of bloom and flower color vary according to cultivar, but figure on anything from creamy white to crimson, beginning in February and sometimes lasting till May. The glaucous, blue-black fruits are attractive, but are strictly survival food for humans, although birds are fond of them.

'Elk River Red' is a tried-and-true Oregon variety that blesses many a Portland garden. At the Gardens of Elk Rock at Bishop's Close, this currant's sizzling color stops the heart and the eye. It's quite an exclamation point in a landscape resplendent in early

R. sanguineum 'Pulborough Scarlet'

spiketail (*Stachyurus praecox*, one of the finest specimens of its kind) and buttercup winter hazel *(Corylopsis pauciflora)* as it floats in a pond of blue *Pulmonaria* blooms.

It's arguable whether, within their given color range, *R. sanguineum* cultivars are strikingly different. Not that local nurseries can keep any of them in stock. The most accessible red forms are the aforementioned 'King Edward', more compact than most, and 'Pulborough Scarlet', another rich-blooded import and an extremely reliable bloomer. Opinion is divided as to whether these two cultivars are tougher than those bred closer to home; all in all, none of the cultivars seem to sniff at 0°F. We lose a little in hardiness but gain enormously in matters sublime when the subject is *Ribes speciosum*. If you're a fuchsia lover and have been suffering winter withdrawal, this gooseberry's the next best thing. Native to coastal California (and therefore quite tolerant of heat and drought, though it will die back to the ground at 12°F), this spiny-stemmed shrub has an arching, twiggy habit, reaching four feet high and six feet wide. It has bite-sized lobed leaves and slender, dangling fuchsia-red flowers with spidery-legged stamens, shown off to best advantage espaliered against a south-facing wall of a contrasting color.

One more early-flowering currant: *Ribes laurifolium*, a native of China, with drooping racemes that are the ultimate in chartreuse, enhanced by leathery, evergreen foliage with reddish maroon stems. It tops out at three feet, takes shade and a variety of soils, and should make a splash combined with plum-stained hellebores, tucked under larger shrubs.

That's my opinion, anyway; to be certain, you'd better check with my mom.

Ribes sanguineum

Rhododendron lutescens

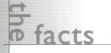

the facts

BOTANICAL NAME:
Rhododendron lutescens

SOUNDS LIKE:
Rhododendron
you peasants

TYPE:
Wide, open, and airy yel-
low-flowered broadleaf
evergreen, 9 feet

BASIC NEEDS:
Part to full sun; well-
drained soil

WORST ENEMY:
The thousands of other
genus-mates that steal
its thunder

BEST ADVICE:
Buy *R. lutescens* in flower if
your heart's set on char-
treuse rather than yellow

For me, writing about rhododendrons is like Woody Allen making a film about sexual abstinence. He neither practices it nor gets the point. But that's not to say he might not admire the concept and wouldn't give it a brief try.

Well, on that point, maybe I'm stretching it.

Now that I've been delivered from Rhododendron Purgatory, the weevil-notched, root-rotted Southeast, I really am looking forward to giving rhodies a try. My notes from the Crystal Springs Rhodo-dendron Garden have big asterisks around the name, *R. macabeanum* (I call it the Hanukkah bush: Judah Maccabee—get it?), which stopped me in my tracks with its massive leaves and their white woolly undersides. But that was in May; otherwise, I'd have taken a Magic Marker to the name *R. lutescens*, a warm splash of sunlight in the late-winter garden with all the promise of daffodils in spring.

The earliest of the yellows to bloom in the maritime Northwest, this widely variable species is the epitome of subtlety, in translucent colors ranging from chartreuse through soft yellow.

The multiple bud trusses are made up of relatively small individ-ual flowers, typical of other rhodies in this triflora subsection (which also boasts the too-blue-to-be-believed *R. augustinii*). Yet despite the quieter, ethereal quality of its flowers, *R. lutescens* in bloom emanates waves of light and energy, largely because the sur-rounding landscape has yet to emerge from its winter funk (admit-tedly, I could be projecting here).

Unlike the many dense, stiff, glossy-leaved rhodies, *R. lutescens* has an airy, billowing form, with light green leaves that emerge bronze and retain a red tint to their edges in ample sun. Though they are evergreen, a dark background—perhaps your existing rhodie hedge—will go a long way toward showing off the shrub in leaf and particularly in flower.

Lucie Sorensen, proprietor of The Bovees Nursery in Portland,

Oregon, and a doyenne worthy of the name, has some unexpected advice about *R. lutescens*: Grow it in sun. Not how you'd expect to treat such a pale beauty, but Sorensen insists it will be more compact, will bloom more heavily, and—could it be?—once established, will not need supplemental summer water. I've also seen them growing happily in filtered light. So if you're looking out your window in late winter and notice that nothing is blooming, it's the time to renounce abstinence and bring home a precocious shrub.

gimme more

It's a crumb, I know, but for you lovers of chartreuse flowers, check out the species *R. keiskei* and its offspring 'Shamrock'.

R. lutescens

Rhododendron lutescens

Salix melanostachys

DECIDUOUS SHRUB

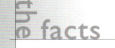
When I first began the study of plants, I was an impressionable student. Never mind that I was over thirty-five. So when I ended up taking classes from a particularly dynamic and opinionated teacher—and one with a *wicked* sense of humor—I gobbled up every word he said.

I found myself thinking about Phil Normandy the other day as I sat down to write about pussy willows (now, don't go jumping to any conclusions). I remember a sunny, late-winter morning at a public garden as we stood around and stamped our cold feet, listening to Phil make cracks about *Salix caprea,* everybody's favorite fuzzy willow.

"Cuteness alert," he warned, "Essentially, it's trash. Don't plant it." I remain constitutionally incapable of recommending *S. caprea* (ditto, Kwanzan cherry and Skyrocket juniper). Thanks, Phil.

But I'm willing to strike out on my own as regards *Salix melanostachys,* the black pussy willow, which my mentor recently described as "not something I'd fall over dead to have." Granted, it's no lacebark pine, but it is strikingly catkined, easily accommodated, and not remotely cute. We're talking serious nonconformism, with a little mystery and wonder on the side, because even when it's the color of a pansy, there's nothing adorable about black.

Imagine, then, that you've been watching a multi-stemmed, five-foot shrubful of vertically aligned buds swell for a couple of weeks. One bright, warm, late winter day, a number of them burst open and shed their boring brownness. Out pop fuzzy catkins, as on many willows, but this time they're of the deepest dye, one- to two-inch spiked inflorescences made up of tiny dark flower scales.

S. melanostachys

By the time you get out for a closer look, the shrub's been touched by that old black magic: Orange-red anthers are bursting out of the catkins like clowns tumbling out of a VW bug. Further along in the act, the opening anthers glow yellow with shedding pollen, and because the process is staggered, you're watching the entire spectacle from black to bursting on one single purplish stem. _S. melanostachys_ (syn. _S. gracilistyla_ var. _melanostachys_) is particularly extraordinary at a time when the leaf buds of other plants are just breaking. As the season progresses, its foliage is certainly attractive—elliptical, heavily ribbed, dark green above and sort of bluish underneath. The plant's shape is upright and its need for space modest; with this willow, at any rate, your plumbing is not at risk.

However, there's no getting around the fact that it has only one truly stellar season, as glorious as those few weeks may be. To make the most of them, site it for maximum impact; consider it as a winter patio plant. Better yet, if you can spare an out-of-the-way spot with full sun and ample moisture, bring out the vases and send in the clowns.

gimme more

Here are a few unusually delicious small willows:

S. helvetica:
Small, silvery green leaves with white undersides, silver-yellow catkins; to 2 feet

S. hastata 'Wehrhahnii':
Bright green leaves, silvery gray catkins, chocolate gray bark; to 3 feet

Salix melanostachys

Sarcococca

BROADLEAF EVERGREEN

Procrastination is a beautiful thing, particularly when in the guise of research. This morning, for instance, I killed a righteous few hours comparing the foliage of five kinds of sweet box, *Sarcococca,* a genus renowned for its winter fragrance. Witness the results:

S. hookerana var. *humilis* has leaves that are medium glossy and tapered, while those of *S. confusa* are long, slender, and richly lustrous. *S. saligna* has distinctively narrow, lance-shaped leaves, while those of *S. ruscifolia* var. *chinensis,* though also dark and shiny, undulate. However, there's no mistaking any of them for *S. hookerana* var. *digyna,* whose gray-green leaves, borne on upright branches, are slim and polished.

Hello, what's that you say about the Emperor's new clothes? Oh, they're green?

That's about the size of it when the subject's sarcococca, regardless of the species. We're talking about a handsome, glossy mound of evergreen foliage, an ideal accent shrub or groundcover that catches light and casts shadows when positioned at the edge of a shaded bed. Though some leaves are slightly more elegant than others, species are most readily told apart by size (if it's five feet, it's *S. confusa,* the biggest of the lot). Another giveaway is berry color: *S. ruscifolia's* summer fruit is red.

This last species makes a dense, three- to four-foot stand of arching stems which, by January, are punctuated by tiny, spidery white flowers. The foliage is somewhat more undulating (here we go again) and overall, the plant's pretty rugged; once established, it can take dryish shade. Word on the block, however, is that it does tend to defoliate after bloom (not to worry, the leaves grow back), though it's easily root-hardy above 0°F.

If hardiness is your current obsession and your primary shopping criterion, there's only one sarcococca for you: *S. hookerana* var. *humilis* (syn. *S. humilis*). At temperatures below 0°F, this plant remains unscathed (it's hardy to –20°F, but its looks will be considerably marred). Small and slow-growing, this naturally occurring variety spreads much like *Pachysandra* (same plant family), and could be used as a discriminating alternative to that overused plant. Like those of all sarcococcas, its winter flowers are inconspicuous, so you're never quite sure at first of the source of its heady honey scent.

To get the most from this species, give it richly amended, loose soil to encourage its spread. It doesn't need to be massed to be effective; you can just use it for a spot of high gloss. With any of the plants in this delicious genus, be sure they're sited where their scent beckons like a curled index finger, lifting you off your feet and on toward mystery like a floating figure in a Chagall.

S. hookerana var. *humilis*

gimme more

S. hookerana var. digyna (syn. S. digyna):
Most fragrant form; grayish-green foliage, purpleblushed stems, and pinktinged flowers. 3 feet high; to 0°F.

Senecio

EVERGREEN SHRUB

S. 'Sunshine'

You gotta love Latin. It's so human.

Case in point: The huge genus *Senecio,* a member of the daisy family. Its name is rooted in the Latin *senex,* for "old man," though the genus is neither stooped, frail, crochety, nor inherently wise. The story's much more homespun than that.

Turns out that once upon a time, a botanist gazed upon the plant's fluffy, white seed heads and was reminded of his own grandfather's head of wiry, silver-gray hair. The suggestion was so strong, the botanist borrowed the image to give the plant its Latin name.

Charming, no? So what if I made it up, the explanation's entirely plausible. What is true is that the "old man" reference has been knocking around since the first century A.D., when the great naturalist Pliny made note of the plant's hoary senescent flowers.

The huge genus includes annuals, perennials, shrubs, and vines, though English garden writer William Robinson dismisses most of them as worthless weeds. You've probably run into a few senecios in your time, including golden ragwort *(Senecio aureus)*, or that tiny

BOTANICAL NAME:
Senecio

SOUNDS LIKE:
Denise he know

TYPE:
Mounding, wider than tall, yellow-flowering evergreen shrub, to 4 feet

BASIC NEEDS:
Full sun, good drainage

WORST ENEMY:
Compacted soil, single-digit temperatures

BEST ADVICE:
A little nip and tuck every spring keeps it from sprawling

chrysanthemum impostor, groundsel *(S. vulgaris)*, or then again that star of the silver screen, 'Dusty Miller' *(S. cineraria)*, limited though her talents may be.

But senecio's status in the hort world reaches new heights with the New Zealand hybrid 'Sunshine', a tough, evergreen shrub that thrives in the Northwest and brings a great, gray calm to the garden. It's one of the Dunedin Hybrids, a cross between three species *(S. greyi, S. compactus,* and *S. laxifolius)*, though hardier than each of its parents. It's got a compact, knee- to thigh-high, upright bouncy bearing quieted by a coat of whitish down. Only the leaf tops are dark green; the rest of the plant is luminescent, not unlike the color of lamb's ears without so much fuzz. The down never fades, and it provides a brilliant contrast to the leaf surface even when the skies are leaden gray.

S. 'Sunshine' is said to resent wet weather and to need excellent drainage. Yet I've seen plants flourish in reasonably amended though not gravelly soil, and noticed they've been undefeated by excessive rain. The plant does have a tendency to sprawl, but spread is easy to contain if you shear the sides back each year (do so late enough in spring, and you might even avoid its weeny yellow composite flowers).

A final word about the humanity of Latin: Since we're a species known to err, it's not exactly news that we often confuse the names of plants. For one thing, 'Sunshine' has been consistently misrepresented in the trade as *Senecio greyi*, so if you bought the latter, you could have the hybrid instead.

Better yet, depending on the authority, 'Sunshine' and its parent species are not *Senecio* at all, but are instead listed as members of the genus *Brachyglottis* (from the Greek "short tongue," referring to the size of the florets).

It's enough to give you white hair.

Uncinia

EVERGREEN ORNAMENTAL GRASS

Every leaf I've longed for lately has come from down under. Whether they're arched and strapping (as in *Phormium*), dime-sized and silver-plated *(Corokia)*, or glossed and undulating *(Pittosporum)*, I can almost predict the encyclopedia will read "New Zealand, Zone 8."

So when I found out that my latest heartthrob, *Uncinia unciniata* (red hook sedge), was also from New Zealand, I rejoiced, because a hardiness rating of give or take 15°F makes me feel snug.

I realize the same information might make another gardener shudder. But after an accurate assessment of the zone I live in (Portland, for instance, is a solid Zone 8), our willingness to take risks—if we even perceive it as that—finally comes down to how badly we want the plant.

So here comes my sales pitch to those of you who live in regions that have never known the pleasures of a Kiwi-colored frost.

It's early November in your garden. Yawn. Autumnal debris covers most of your low perennials, and if it weren't for those purple heucheras, you'd have no color at all. But imagine this: Reaching out of the mess are several calf-high grassy mounds, each leaf blade as glossy as licorice, deeply brunette, and brushed with an olive sheen. Good color, sturdy habits, and clearly not on the wane.

Six weeks later, mid-December. Is that a garden or a label graveyard? Good thing you finally tried all that black mondo grass, along with your *Heuchera* 'Pewter Veil'. Now imagine that those same grassy mounds have turned a rich mahogany, sweetened with an orange glaze. How clever of you to mix them in among your silvery purples and lustrous blacks!

Not a bad trick for a plant, turning its brightest colors when the weather gets cold, whether bronze, ochre, copper,

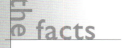

the facts

BOTANICAL NAME:
Uncinia

SOUNDS LIKE:
Sun city ya

COMMON NAME:
Red hook sedge

TYPE:
Evergreen grass,
to 18 inches

BASIC NEEDS:
Sun, good drainage

WORST ENEMY:
Temperatures that
near single digits

BEST ADVICE:
Winter protection or
toast, your choice

***U. rubra* (orange hook sedge):**
Typically, similar to
U. uncinata

U. egmontiana:
Brilliant orange to copper winter color; under
1 foot

or brilliant red. In that way, red hook sedge functions in the garden much like *Carex testacea*, a larger, thinner-bladed grass that spends winter as a glowing orange globe. More compact and glossier than *Carex*, this evergreen sedge is happiest in sun, and must have well-drained soil that does not dry out during summer. You won't necessarily kill it without water, but it will get shabby, and its winter color won't be nearly as showy. Come spring, if it gets a little ragged, you can either prune it lightly or cut it way back and have a restored plant by summer.

Should you come across this little beauty in the nursery before the end of summer, by all means take it home. That way it will have ample time to settle in before the cold winds of doubt start to blow. Otherwise, hold off ordering and planting till spring.

U. uncinata

Index

a-b

index

t-z